NATIVE LIFE IN INDIA

NATIVE LIFE IN INDIA

BEING

Sketches of the Social and Religious Characteristics of the Hindus

BY THE

REV. HENRY RICE

GYAN

Published by

Gyan Publishing House
5, Ansari Road
Daryaganj, New Delhi-110002
Phone: 011-47034999, 9811692060
E-mail: books@gyanbooks.com

Distribution Network
gyanbooks.com
India, USA, Canada, UK, Australia, France

ISBN: 978-81-212-8005-1 (PB)
First Published, 1891

2nd Impression 2023

Printed at: Gyan Press, Delhi.

NATIVE LIFE IN INDIA
Author: HENRY RICE

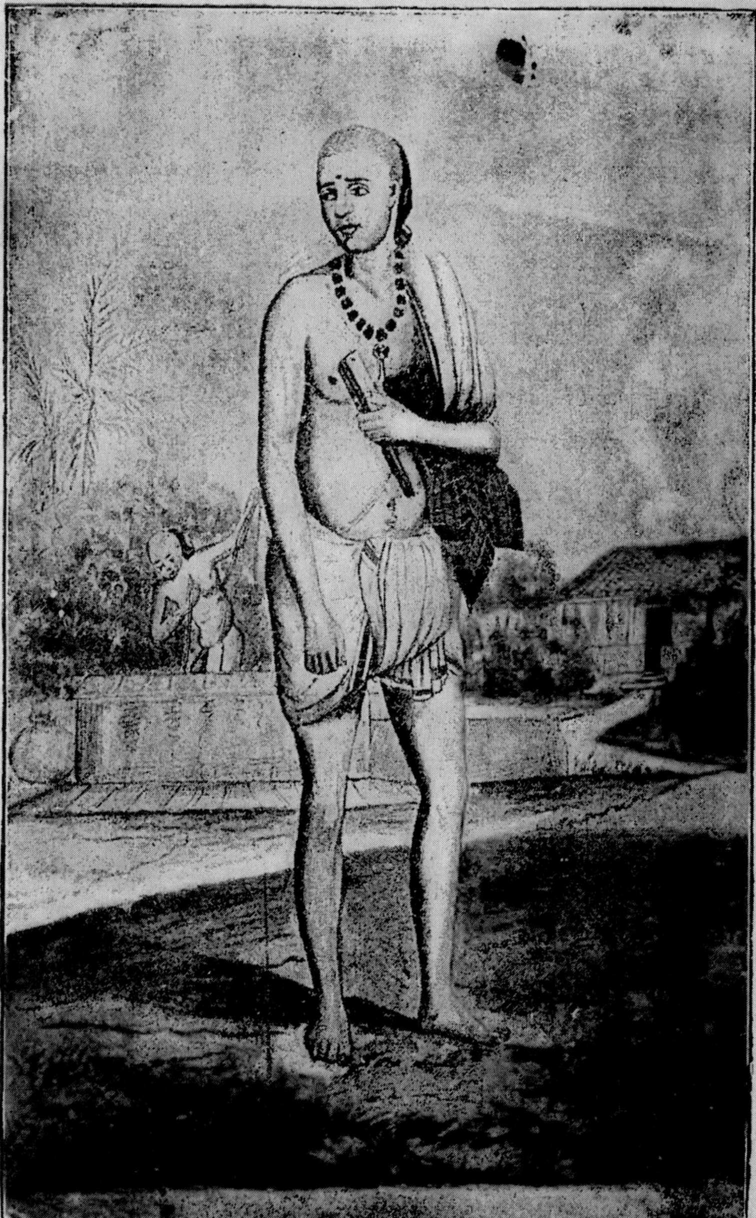

A BRAHMIN.

(From a native drawing.)

NATIVE LIFE IN INDIA

BEING

Sketches of the Social and Religious Characteristics of the Hindus

---

BY THE

REV. HENRY RICE

MADRAS

REVISED

PACIFIC PRESS PUBLISHING COMPANY

OAKLAND, CAL.

SAN FRANCISCO, NEW YORK, LONDON

PREFACE.

HAVING for upwards of eighteen years moved freely among all classes of the people in various parts of India, and having taken notes of what I have seen and heard, I have ventured to put them together in this little book. Many of these pages, especially those on the manners and customs of the people, have been read over to an educated Brahmin of good family and position, who vouches for their general accuracy. For what has not come directly under my own observation I am indebted to other sources, especially to Dr. Cornish's invaluable Census Report. To all such I desire to express my obligations.

In no part of the world, perhaps, is it truer that what is said of one part of the country may not be equally applicable to another. I have, therefore, only incidentally alluded to Mysore and Travancore, as the manners and customs of the people of those provinces are in many respects different from those of the other parts of South India. As regards Travancore, there is an admirable book on the subject, entitled "The Land of Charity," by my esteemed friend, the Rev. S. Mateer, of Trevandrum. As regards Mysore, a popular account of the present-day life of the people has, I believe, still to be written. I have also alluded only briefly to the Mohammedans, as they do not strictly come under the scope of the title of this little book.

That the perusal of these pages may lead to increased interest in the people of South India, and to more earnest and enlarged efforts for their evangelization, is my sincere desire and fervent prayer.

HENRY RICE.

PUBLISHERS' NOTE.

IN the present increase of interest in foreign missions, the publishers take pleasure in presenting to the public, as one of the volumes of the YOUNG PEOPLE'S LIBRARY, the following pages. The book was first published by the Religious Tract Society of London. The matter and cuts have been purchased by the present publishers for America. The title, "Native Life in South India," has been changed to the more euphonious and shorter term, "Native Life in India." The book, however, does not include all of South India, as stated in the author's preface; but as it treats of the more important part of India, and as the system of caste is similar in principle throughout the country, this work gives the reader a general idea of Indian customs, manners, and religions. In the revision of the work the object has been to simplify, for the benefit of the young. But very little has been omitted—in one instance a page nearly of Indian words which might possibly satisfy the curiosity of the learned, but would be of no benefit to the general reader; in a few other instances some of the author's opinions, comparisons, and conclusions concerning the conversion, or Christianizing, of India, which, to the publishers, do not seem to be warranted by the Scriptures of truth. Not one fact, however, pertaining to the subject matter of the book, has been omitted, and it is believed that the conservative revision which the book has undergone and the form in which it is presented to the public will render it more interesting to the reader, and of greater advantage to the purchaser, than the original work. To some readers the first three chapters, pertaining to the geographical features of the country and the various castes, may be dry and prosy, but it is sincerely hoped that they will proceed, for the book grows continually more interesting. That it may arouse within the readers' hearts stronger desires and purposes to help enlighten those who are in the darkness of error, is the prayer of THE PUBLISHERS.

CONTENTS.

ILLUSTRATIONS.

Native Life in India.

BEING

SKETCHES OF THE SOCIAL AND RELIGIOUS CHARACTERISTICS OF THE HINDUS.

CHAPTER I.

SOME GEOGRAPHICAL, CLIMATIC, AND LINGUISTIC CHARACTERISTICS OF THE MADRAS PRESIDENCY.

THE Madras presidency occupies, with its dependencies and the States of Mysore, the entire southern part of the peninsula of India, or Hindustan. On the east it extends from Orissa, in Bengal, to Cape Comorin. On the west the narrow strip of country which includes the native states of Travancore and Cochin, forms the coast line from Cape Comorin to the town of Cochin, where Madras territory again extends along the coast until its junction with the Bombay presidency, at the northern extremity of the South Canara district. In the center are the Nagpore country and Berar, the territories of the Nizam, known as the Deccan, and the province of Mysore; but all the center of the peninsula south and east of Mysore belongs to the Madras presidency.

Its extreme length is about nine hundred and fifty miles, and its extreme breadth about four hundred and fifty. It consists of three classes of territory: (1) The twenty-two British districts; (2) the agency tracts of Ganjam, Vizagapatam, and Godavari, under a special administration; and (3) the five native States in political dependence on the Madras Government, viz., Travancore, Cochin, Pudukota, Banganapalli, and Sandur. Including the agency tracts and the native States, the territory under the Madras Government (1881) contains an area of one hundred and forty-nine thousand and ninety-two square miles, with a population of thirty-four million one hundred and seventy-two thousand and sixty-seven persons, dwelling in fifty-seven thousand and twenty-two towns and villages.

The peculiar physical feature of the presidency is a long mountain range running from north to south along the western coast, called the Western Ghauts. These hills arrest the rain clouds blown up from the Indian Ocean by the periodical winds of the southwest monsoon, and cause excessive rainfall on the narrow strip of coast on the west side. The heaviest rainfall on the eastern coast, especially in the southeast, takes place during the northeast monsoon. During this monsoon, when the eastern coast is deluged with rain, the western coast enjoys fine, clear weather, all caused by the western range of mountains, which has a similar effect in arresting the rain clouds from passing over. Along the eastern coast, again, run the Eastern Ghauts, until they lose themselves in the Neilgherries, and there unite with the western range. The highest point of the Neilgherries is Doddabetta, more than eight thousand feet high. Here the traveler from the heated plains can enjoy cool and invigorating breezes amid romantic scenery of hills, lakes, and waterfalls. This region is inhabited by a shepherd race, called Todahs, having strange customs and speaking a peculiar dialect. There are other outlying spurs and hills, chief of which are the Shevaroys in Salem, the Anamallis in Coimbatoor, and the Pulneys in Madura.

The varied physical features of Southern India cause considerable differences of climate in various parts of the presidency. The Neilgherry Hills enjoy the climate of the temperate zone, with a temperature rarely exceeding 80° Fahr. On the Malabar coast, during the prevalence of the southwest monsoon, the sun is sometimes obscured for months together, and rainfall is very great, amounting in some places to one hundred and fifty inches in the year. On the eastern coast and on the central table-lands, however, the rainfall is comparatively slight and the heat in the dry season excessive. The average rainfall in the city of Madras is about forty-nine inches a year, but this is considerably above the average of the east coast generally. The coolest months in Madras are November, December, January, and a portion of February. The hottest months are April, May, and June. September is close and steamy, and often one of the most trying months in the year. But, although the hot weather is the least agreeable, it is frequently the healthiest time of the year. The east coast is subject to destructive cyclones, which frequently destroy the shipping and overflow the low-lying ports.

The city of Madras is ordinarily healthy either for natives or Europeans. The temperature is high all the year round, but there are fewer sudden changes of heat and cold than in most places in India. The death rate is thirty-three per thousand. It usually increases during the cold and rainy reason, and is at its least during the dry, hot months of April, May, and June.

Properly speaking, there are only two seasons in the year—the dry and the rainy, produced by the periodical winds called monsoons. There is no spring, summer, autumn, or winter, as the trees are never stripped of their leaves, and flowers are always in blossom. There is no reason, however, why a person possessing a good constitution, and living an active, temperate life, with moderation in eating and drinking, and avoidance of chills, over-fatigue,

A HIGH CASTE HINDU WOMAN.

(From a native dr..wing.)

etc., should not live as long there as in any other part of the world.

The chief food grains are rice, *cholam* (a kind of maize), *cumboo* (a kind of millet), and *ragi* and *gingelly* (oil seeds); the principal garden crops are chillies, tobacco, sugar cane, plantains, and betel-leaf. The trees mostly grown are cocoanut, areca-nut, jack, tamarind, and mango.

The diseases mostly prevalent are cholera, fever, small-pox, diarrhea, dysentery, bowel complaints, and various forms of inflammation. Amongst the natives scrofula, elephantiasis, leprosy, and ophthalmia are very common.

As regards language, the Madras presidency is inhabited almost exclusively by a single family of the human race, called Dravidian, who speak the Tamil and its kindred languages—the Telu, Tulugu, Canarese, and Malayalam. Even the Brahmins, the most important of the classes who have intermixed with the population, but who represent a different element, have adopted the Dravidian language. The word Dravida is probably a Sanscrit one, and is now employed to indicate the languages peculiar to the south and southeast of the peninsula. Early Sanscrit writers called the languages of South India the Andhradravidabasha, the language of the Andhras and Dravidas, or of the Telugus and Tamulians. Canarese was included in Andhra, and Malayalam in Dravida. The inhabitants of the extreme south, and those shut in by the mountains of the western coast, exhibit peculiarities which are probably older than those of any other civilized community in the world.

With reference to the age of the Dravidian languages nothing definite is known. Tamil literature does not carry the language back beyond the ninth or tenth century A. D., but Greek writings trace it to the beginning of the Christian era. Several primitive Dravidian words are found in the early Greek and Latin geographers. It is probable that the Dravidian languages are older in point of time than the Sanscrit, and that they have been driven to the south and along the east coast by the encroachment of other languages from the northwest. After the immigration of the Aryans, the Dravidians borrowed words from the Sanscrit to express abstract ideas of philosophy, science, and religion; but the original language was not radically altered. The new words were regarded rather as luxuries than as necessaries. In the speech of the Brahmins and more learned Tamulians, Sanscrit words are largely used, but a Tamil poetical composition is regarded as classical in proportion as it omits Sanscrit words

Without entering minutely into the peculiarities of the language, some of its more prominent features may be briefly noticed. The Tamil language has two dialects, the high and the low. The former is the language of the poets and of all elegant prose writings. The two differ greatly, and a person may be acquainted with the one without knowing the other. The language numbers thirty letters, viz., twelve vowels and eighteen consonants. The vowel is called *ooyir*, life or soul; and the consonant *mey*, body. There are no aspirates. The most difficult consonants are *zh*, *r*, and *l*. Very few Europeans can pronounce these letters accurately. The classical, or high, dialect is called *shen* Tamil, or elegant Tamil, while the latter is called *kodun* Tamil, or rough or common Tamil, and is the language spoken by the people.

The consonant *ch* represents all sibilants. The words are written from left to right, as in English, and in native books they are printed without any separation, which is often very perplexing.

The word "Tamil" means "melodiousness," denoting the high estimation in which the language is held. No language combines greater force and brevity, or is more close and philosophic in its modes of expression, while the various degrees of rank and station are provided for by the use of different pronouns. Altogether there are, it is estimated, about twenty-nine million speaking the Dravidian languages. Tamil is spoken by about twelve million three hundred and eighty-eight thousand persons; Telugu, by twelve million one hundred and five thousand; Malayalam, by two million three hundred and seventy thousand; Canarese, by one million three hundred thousand five hundred and fifty-five; Tulu, by four hundred and twenty-seven thousand; Khond, by two hundred and five thousand; Gond, by eight thousand. The Tamil language, probably, shows the greatest tendency to spread. Some words of Tamil origin have been incorporated into the English language, such as "cheroots," from the Tamil *shiruttu*, a roll; "cot" from the Tamil *kattile*, and others.

CHAPTER II.

CASTES AND SECTS.

The Priesthood—The Warrior Caste—The Trading Caste—The Agricultural Caste—The Shepherd Caste—The Artisan Caste.

THE division of Hindu society into castes is the most striking peculiarity of its social life, and has no parallel in any other country in the world. It defines what a man must do, and what he must not do; it determines by a code of its own what actions are good and what are bad; it shows far greater respect for its own harsh rules than for the laws of morality; it insists on a blind adherence to the past, and is thus the most conservative national power in the whole world, as well as a vast instrument for good or for evil. The entire system is despotic and tyrannical, and punishes all who disregard its rules, by cutting them off from society. It is a very different thing from the social distinctions which prevail in English society. The pride of birth, the pride of wealth, aristocratic pride, ecclesiastical pride, do exist in England, but there caste is an ugly growth by no means essential to the national life, while in India it is a part and parcel of it. Without it Hindu society would break up, and is in fact breaking up wherever its power is diminishing. It forbids a Hindu to eat and drink with a foreigner, or to have any intimate relations with him.

Theoretically, the Hindus are divided into four great castes, viz., Brahmins, or priests; Rajpoots, called also Kshatriyas, the military class; Vaisyas, or merchants, bankers, and traders; and Sudras, or agriculturists, artisans, shepherds, etc. But practically every separate trade, profession, or occupation constitutes a distinct caste. Every caste, moreover, has its subdivisions, which are generally as socially disconnected as if they were separate castes. The people mix together in the streets, in trade, and are to a certain extent on friendly terms with one another, but socially they are as distinct as though they belonged to different worlds. They cannot intermarry, or eat and drink together. The different sections of Hindu society are so many, and the traditions and sentiments of each so distinct, that one caste is comparatively little influenced by any movement taking place in another. A clear understanding of the various caste divisions among the people is a matter of some difficulty. We have several times asked educated men of good social position to explain the various divisions and subdivisions prevailing among the people, but have found that they themselves do not understand the subject. The following classification of the different castes as they exist in South India may be regarded as substantially correct:—

(1) Brahmins, the priesthood; (2) Kshatriyas, the warrior caste; (3) Chetties, the trading caste; (4) Vellalars, the agricultural caste; (5) Idaiyar, the shepherd caste; (6) Kammalan, the artisan caste; (7) Kanakkan, the writer or accountant caste; (8) Kaikalar, the weaver caste; (9) Vunniar or Pullie, the agricultural laboring caste; (10) Kusaven, the potter caste; (11) Satani, the mixed caste; (12) Sembadaven, the fishing and hunting caste; (13) Shanars, the palm-cultivating caste; (14) Ambattan, the barber caste; (15) Vannan, the washerman caste; (16) the Pariahs or out-castes.

The Brahmins belong to the Aryan race, and came into South India about the beginning of the Christian era. They are fair-featured, handsome, and well-built, courtly and polished in their manners, but very haughty and crafty. The Brahmins of South India are largely worshipers of Shiva, but there are also followers of Vishnu and Linga among them. They are divided into three classes according to their religious philosophy. The Smartas are followers of Sarkaracharya and worshipers of Shiva. They are Adwaitas in philosophy, that is, they believe that the soul of man and the soul of God are identical. The Madhwas are followers of Madhwacharya, and worshipers of Vishnu. In philosophy they are Dwaitas, that is, they believe that the soul of man and the soul of God are distinct. The Sri Veishnavas follow the teachings of Ramanujacharyar and worship Vishnu. They are called Visishta-Adwaitas, or "Adwaitas with a difference," because they hold that while the divine and human souls are in some respects identical, yet that in life the human soul is subordinate to the divine soul. The chief duties of a Brahmin are to read and teach the Vedas, to perform sacrifices for himself and for others. He is forbidden to live by service, but on alms. It is the duty of people to support him liberally, and at all religious ceremonies they are feasted and sent away with presents. But the Brahmins of the present day have largely departed from the rule of life laid down for them. Large numbers of them are employed in the government service; some are lawyers, others are Purohitas, or family priests, while a considerable proportion are landholders. This land, which has generally been given to their ancestors by some native prince, is frequently the best in the country, and is cultivated by serf labor with little or no effort on their part. They are divided into Gotrams, or clans, according to the country from which they originally migrated. They are cleanly in their person, and, as a rule, strict vegetarians and teetotalers; but in large towns and among the educated young men strong drinks are becoming common, while some also eat flesh. The Brahmins cremate their dead, and their widows are not allowed to remarry. They never worship the village deities, as the abo-

AN OIL MILL.

(From a native drawing.)

See page 27.

riginal races do. In Malabar the Brahmins are called Namburis, and are a fine, handsome race of men.

The Kshatriya, or warrior caste, is also called Rajput, which signifies "sons of kings," and implies their descent from ancient rajahs. They have all come from the north, and, except in Tinnevelly, where there is a large colony of them, are not found to any large extent in South India. Some few are employed in the military service of the government, while others are *zeminders*, owning estates and living on the income derived therefrom. In their customs they approximate largely to the Brahmins, and wear the sacred thread as they do.

The Chetties, or trading castes, are an important section of the community. They care little for government service, and confine themselves almost exclusively to trade and mercantile pursuits. They have a keen eye to business, and their sole ambition is to get money and become rich. There are several subdivisions among them, two of which are the bankers and money lenders of the people. They are, generally speaking, fair-complexioned, and their money transactions are on a large scale. Their drafts are seldom dishonored, and they lend out money at high rates of interest.

One of these subdivisions is the oil pressers. The seed is placed in a hollow wooden mortar into which the grinder and presser fit. This grinder is turned by a long beam, to which is yoked one or two oxen. The oil is thus pressed, and the operation, which may be seen in almost any village, makes a disagreeable grating sound, and is heard at a long distance.

The bazaar, or shop-man, sits crosslegged in the midst of his wares in his shop, which is quite open to the street, and situated in the most frequented thoroughfares.

The Vellalars, or Agricultural caste, forms the backbone of the country, and is by far the most numerous in the presidency. Under this name are included several subdivisions. The Vellalars may be taken as representative of the cultivating caste in the Tamil-speaking districts of South India. They take the title *Mudali* (chief man), and in some districts *Pillai* (sons of the gods), which is used also by the shepherd and accountant castes.

The agricultural laborer may be seen in early morning in every village of India, going forth to his labor, carrying on his shoulder his yoke and plow, which he steadies with one hand, while with the other he holds the rope reins fastened to his tiny bullocks. The plow consists of two rude sticks with an iron spike at the end, which constitutes the share. This he guides with one hand, while with the other he guides the cattle, and thus makes a rut or scratch in the field. The seed is sown in various ways. Sometimes while the field is being plowed for the last time a man walks behind and drops the seed into the furrow. At other times a long tube is attached to the plow; while the plow is moving forward the man who holds it drops the seed into the tube at the upper end, and it falls into the furrow at the other end. A third method is to carry the seed in a basket and scatter by the hand over the surface of the field.

There are two kinds of cultivation of the soil, wet and dry; the former is used for rice and indigo, the land being watered by tanks or lakes, with high embankments, or from deep wells. The latter mode of cultivation is adopted for sugar-cane, wheat, barley, fruits, and vegetables. When the grain appears in the ear, it is watched night and day, to protect it from thieves and birds. If the grain has grown so high that the whole field cannot be taken in at a glance, small platforms are erected, consisting of four poles stuck in the ground, with a framework of bamboos placed on them. On these platforms boys or women are stationed, who continually call out, to frighten away the birds. When the grain is ripe, it is reaped and spread out in the open air in a clean part of the field. Some grains are threshed by driving round and round upon them four or five bullocks abreast. Contrary to the Scripture injunction, the bullocks are muzzled. When the stalks have been sufficiently trodden, they take baskets full of the grain, and, standing in a certain position, when there is a slight breeze blowing, drop it down slowly. The wind separates the husk from the grain, the latter falling at the feet of the man, the former being blown away. This is their method of winnowing, or cleaning, the grain. When all is finished, part of it is kept for their own use, and a part of it is sold to pay the government tax. After a field has been reaped, the poor are allowed to come and pick up what remains.

The farmers generally occupy small farms, which they hold direct from the State. Their standing is known by the number of pairs of bullocks they keep and the number of plows they use. If he is a poor man, he can only keep one pair of bullocks and cultivate a small piece of land. If he is a wealthy man, he cultivates a larger piece, and in addition to having four or five pairs of bullocks he keeps two or three cows and buffaloes, which supply him with an abundance of milk; his women are adorned with gold and silver ornaments, and he has a large number of brass cooking utensils in his house. The agricultural classes are intensely conservative in all their ways. They never act on their own responsibility, but will only do what "ten men" do. Blind devotion to ancient custom constitutes their religion, and they deem it as perilous to forsake that as for a locomotive to quit the rails. They are firm fatalists, and believe that every man's destiny is written on his forehead. They are characterized by much simplicity, mingled with great shrewdness of practical wisdom. Although the Vellalars are somewhat behindhand in availing themselves of the benefits of English education, yet they are now proving themselves possessed of considerable mental power. Not a few of the graduates of the Madras University have come from this class.

Idaiyar, the shepherd and pastoral caste, formed an important division of the people in ancient times, before the land was brought under cultivation. It is not improbable that it was supreme all over India in former days, but it now holds a subordinate place to the cultivating class. The word "*idaiyir*" means "middle," that is, neither high nor low class. They keep sheep, goats, milch kine and buffaloes; the breeding of cattle and the sale of milk and curds is in their hands, but they have done nothing to improve the breeds or the food supply of the people. They sell the wool which comes off their sheep, and the he-goats are for sacrifice. Their flocks are generally kept in inclosures in the open field, with dogs to protect them from wolves.

Of the Kammalan, or artisan caste, there are five orders—goldsmith, blacksmith, coppersmith, carpenter, and mason. Hence they are sometimes called *Panchala* (*pancha*, five). The artisan castes have always fought for a higher place in the social scale than that assigned to them by the Brahmins. They wear the sacred thread like the Brahmins, and some of them take the title *achari*, or religious teacher. Their *gurus* (priests) are not Brahmins, but members of their own caste. Their favorite deity is Kamatchiammal, identified with Parvati, the wife of Shiva.

The goldsmith carries his shop about with him. His furnace is an earthen pot, his bellows an iron pipe, and his crucible is made on the spot, and thrown away when no longer needed. The females of India being exceedingly fond of jewels, he finds plenty of employment. The jewelers of Trichinopoly make articles of beautiful workmanship and delicate texture, but they lack finish and novelty of design. There is little or no encouragement for artistic display, as an article is prized more on account of its intrinsic value than on account of its excellency of workmanship.

The blacksmith likewise carries his smithy and tools with him. He soon makes a furnace, and, sitting on the ground, with his attendant apprentice, the bellows blower, with a goatskin in each hand at his side, works in that position. His anvil is a stone, and his apparatus a pair of pincers, hammer, mallet, and file.

The carpenter sits on the ground, and holds the wood between his feet. His tools are the hammer, chisel, and saw. The latter has its teeth set towards the handle, and in an opposite direction to that of an English or American saw. With these simple implements he will make almost any article of furniture exceedingly well, lacking only in finish.

The masons work beautifully in stone, as some of their carvings in their temples bear abundant evidence.

The grand characteristic of all the arts in India is the obvious want of power. The hands do their work well, but there is a want of head. There is little knowledge and no emulation. Each man follows the occupation which his father followed, and does his work in the same way; and thus, though one generation follows another, it is the revolution of one dull wheel, and the appearance is still the same. There have been imitations of European articles made for Europeans; but it is doubtful whether during the last four or five hundred years the native intellect of India has contrived a single tool or machine for the effecting of any native purpose.

CHAPTER III.

CASTES AND SECTS—CONTINUED.

The Writer Caste—The Weaver Caste—The Agricultural Laboring Caste—The Potter Caste—Satani, or Mixed Caste—The Fishing and Hunting Caste—The Palm-Cultivating Caste—The Barber Caste—The Washerman Caste—The Pariahs—Mohammedans.

THE writer, or accountant caste, Kanakkan, is popularly called "Karnam." In the early days of the British occupation of the country they were the agents and interpreters of the East India Company, and the word "*conicopillay*," used in reference to agents of mercantile firms, is a corruption of "*Kannakkan pillay*," a writer or accountant. In every village there are three petty officials,—the Munsiff, who is the head magistrate; the Munigar, whose duty it is to collect and remit the government taxes; and the Kannakkan, who keeps the village accounts. These posts are generally hereditary.

Of the Kaikalar, or weaver caste, there are two kinds—cotton weavers and silk weavers. The silk weavers are called Patnulkars. They are, generally speaking, of a fair complexion, and having originally migrated from Guzerat, speak a Guzerati dialect among themselves. Their weaving is done in a cellar or low basement. The cotton weavers, on the other hand, work in the open air. Men, women, and children all work. The loom consists of four forked sticks stuck in the ground, and two pieces across these sticks, to which the ends of the web are attached. With this simple contrivance the weaver manufactures cloth of fine and delicate texture. The weaving industry, however, is in a precarious state, owing to the importation of English-made goods, and, were it not that the Lancashire manufacturers have not as yet succeeded in turning out machine-made cloths equal in price and durability to those of the hand looms of India, might be in a still worse condition. Many of this caste consequently now follow other pursuits. The weavers have the reputation of being given to drink.

The Vunniar, or Pullie, the agricultural laboring caste, is composed of those who were originally slaves to the Vellalars and Brahmin cultivators; but many of them now own small pieces of land of their own, while others cultivate the lands of the higher classes, and share half the net produce. In this caste may be included the Maravars of Madura and Tinnevelly, and the Kallans, also the Oddars, a laboring tribe of Telugu origin. The latter live in villages by themselves, in little conical-shaped huts like beehives. They are a hardy race, and are employed as the tank diggers and road makers of the country. The Maravars and Kallans were originally a lawless and turbulent people, given up to thieving and fighting, but now pursue peaceable occupations. The Vunnias sometimes attach the title of "Naick" or "Naicker" to their names.

The potter caste is employed in making the common red *chatties* (pots) and other clay vessels so much used in cooking, etc. The potter stands and turns the wheel with a bamboo, shaping the vessel as it turns. In this manner he makes vessels of all shapes and sizes. The articles now made are neither so chaste in design nor so well executed as those in former times, as is evident from the pottery found in the tombs of the Turanian race, who formerly populated India.

The mixed caste consist of various classes who have more or less given up caste restrictions. The Satanis derive their name from Sanatana, one of the disciples of Chaitanya, a religious reformer of the fifteenth century. They are mostly worshipers of Vishnu. Some of them wear a rosary of tulsi beads round their necks. Their peculiarity is that they profess to have given up all caste distinctions, and receive anyone who agrees with them in religious views. These are all, generally speaking, religious mendicants and priests of inferior temples. One order of this caste is that of the *Dasis*, or dancing girls, whose ranks are recruited by the female children of the caste, who are always brought up to the same profession, and by female children of other castes, who are presented to the temple by

A BAZAAR MAN.

(From a native drawing.) *See page 28.*

their parents in fulfillment of some vow. Large numbers are attached to the principal temples, and are maintained by the Brahmin priests.

The fishing and hunting caste are industrious but very illiterate. The northern fishing caste, called Bois, a Telugu people, are the best bearers of burdens in the country.

Shanars are the palmyra cultivators, toddy drawers, and distillers of the country. They climb the trees in an ingenious manner, tap them, and extract the juice, which they boil into coarse sugar, or distill into intoxicating drink called toddy or arrack, a species of rum. They correspond with the Tiyars in Malabar and Travancore, and are specially numerous in Tinnevelly, where large numbers have embraced Christianity and risen greatly in the social scale. They are a hard-working and industrious race. They are clearly of a non-Aryan origin, though they have endeavored to prove that they have descended from one of the higher caste. Many of them, especially among the Christians, are well educated and have taken degrees at the Madras University.

The Ambattan, the barber caste, occupy an important place in the Hindu social system. They may be seen sitting by the roadside shaving the head and face of the customer who sits opposite to them. They are also employed as go-betweens in the arrangement of marriages, feasts, and funerals, and act as masters of ceremonies on these occasions. They are the general news agents. They dabble in medicine, also, and act as musicians on public occasions, beating the tom-tom, a kind of drum. Some barbers attend the male members of certain families, and shave them regularly at stated times They receive in return small sums of money, a piece of cloth at festival times or on occasions of a marriage taking place in the family, and are also paid in grain in time of harvest. Barbers also go about the streets seeking for customers. They do not cry out, but are easily recognized by a small bag wrapped in a cloth which they carry with them, containing one or two razors, a pair of scissors or knife, a small looking-glass, and a small piece of leather on which to sharpen the razors. Their occupation is generally hereditary, and they follow the religious beliefs of the majority of their customers. If the majority are worshipers of Vishnu, they follow that belief; if of Siva, then they follow that. No Hindu shaves himself, nor is shaving ever done in the house or shop, but under a tree or shed, very often in the open street. The whole head is shaved bald, with the exception of a little tuft of hair in the middle at the back of the head, which is usually tied in a knot. Some barbers devote themselves to cleaning ears, which they do with a kind of skewer covered at one end with cotton.

Of the Vannan or washerman caste, each washerman has a certain number of houses for which he washes. He goes from house to house and collects the clothes. When collected they are placed in an earthen tub and saturated in a mixture composed of mineral alkali and common soap. Then they are boiled in a large brass vessel over a slow fire. Afterwards they are taken to a pond or river close by and washed by being well beaten on a stone. This method soon destroys good clothes. If the articles are numerous, or the river some distance, donkeys or small bullocks are employed to carry them. When dry, the clothes of the better classes are ironed, while those of the poor are pounded with a mallet till they are soft and smooth. The washermen do not hesitate to wear the clothes given to them to wash, or else to hire them out to others on marriage occasions and during festivals. The washermen, or *dhobis*, as they are called, are much given to drink.

In addition to the above there are other classes of the population, such as magicians and fortune tellers (Koravers), a nomadic tribe, who pitch their camps near villages in open places. They gather jungle produce, weave baskets, and generally possess asses and cattle. They are great thieves, and are carefully watched by the police. The jugglers (Dommeras) are a similar nomadic tribe, who wander about the country in gangs performing athletic feats.

The Brahmins, or priests, the warriors and traders, are called the "twice-born" castes, and wear the sacred thread across their shoulders. The others are called Sudras, and cannot wear the thread.

Practically speaking, all from the Brahmins to the Artisan caste may be considered to be good castes.

There is a peculiar division of the people in South India into right-hand and left-hand castes. The right-hand castes are called Vadangei, and the left-hand Idangei. The latter includes traders, artisans, oil mongers, weavers, male leather workers, and female Pullies. The former includes agriculturists, writers, and others, silk weavers, male Pullies, Pariahs, and female leather workers. It is, practically, a contest for social precedence between the artisan classes on the one hand, and the agricultural and mercantile classes on the other; but the peculiarity is that the females of the two lower classes take different sides to their husbands.

Outside of every Indian village is a small collection of huts, called *cheri*. This is occupied by Pariahs or out-castes. They are called Pariahs from the Tamil word "*parei*," a drum which they beat on festival occasions. These people cultivate the fields of the other inhabitants. They are a hard-working class, and eat almost anything. They are not cleanly in their habits. There are subdivisions among them, such as Chucklers, who are shoemakers and workers in leather, and Totis, who are scavengers. The priests of the Pariahs are called Valluvars. The Taliyari is the head man, whose duty it is to guard the whole village from thieves, and the Vettiyan, who performs all kinds of menial duties. The domestic servants of European families are mostly Pariahs. It is remarkable that one of the best and most popular poems in the Tamil language, the "Kural," was written by a Pariah called Tiruvalluvar, clearly showing that they were not always as degraded as they now are.

The Mohammedans of the Madras presidency number about one million nine hundred thousand, and are mostly a mixed race, resulting from the intermarriage of the Persian and Arab traders with the women of the country. They have no caste distinctions among them, and may be easily recognized from their mode of dress, shaven head, and cultivation of the beard. They may be divided into two principal classes, one being chiefly engaged in trade, or employed as boatmen and fishermen. Religiously they are divided into Shias and Sunis. The latter consider themselves to be the orthodox followers of Mohammed. They assert the supremacy of Mohammed, and acknowledge the first four califs as his successors. The Shias, on the other hand, acknowledge only Ali as his successor, and reject the first three; they insist on the authority of the Koran, and reject certain traditions supported by the Sunis.

The latter class are chiefly found on the western coast, and are, likewise, a mixed race, resulting from the intermarriage of the Arabs with the native women. Their ranks are largely recruited by conversions from the slave castes of Malabar. They are an industrious but fanatical race.

And thus the population of the whole of India is made up of caste, and division of caste, till almost every man is separate from his brother. How different from the gospel of Christ: "For one is your master, even Christ, and all ye are brethren".

CHAPTER IV.

MANNERS AND CUSTOMS.

Outward Appearance of the Hindus—Sectarian Marks—The Dress of Men and Women—Fondness for Jewelry—Mode of Wearing Hair—Their Method of Visiting Europeans—Forms of Salutation—Houses—Food.

IN outward appearance the Hindus of South India are all shades of complexion. Some are fair, or "red," as they term it; others are of a deep black. The prevailing shade may be said to be a sort of mahogany. As a rule the higher classes are fairer than the lower, but not exclusively so. One of the first things to strike a foreigner in mingling with the people is that they all have some kind of mark inscribed on their forehead. Some have three lines drawn across in the shape of a triangle or trident; others, three horizontal lines, or a small round spot in the center of the forehead about the size of a silver dime or half-dime piece. They are made with a paste of sandal-wood moistened with water. These are sectarian marks, and denote what god the wearer worships. They are put on before partaking of the morning meal, and are generally kept on for the rest of the day. The worshipers of Vishnu are distinguished by the trident mark, and employ for the purpose a kind of white earth called *gopichandana.* The mark itself is called *namam,* and consists of two perpendicular white lines drawn from the root of the hair to the commencement of each eyebrow, and a transverse streak uniting them across the nose, while in the center is a perpendicular streak of red made of turmeric and lime. They have, also, patches of this *gopichandana* with a red streak in the center on the breast and upper part of each arm. The marks are said to represent the shell, discus, club, and lotus which Vishnu bears in his four hands. Sometimes these objects are stamped on the body with wooden stamps. Large *namams* may be seen inscribed on the walls of temples, and smaller ones on the doors of houses. The followers of Madhwacharriar have the same frontal mark, but instead of a red line down the center, have a black one made with charcoal. Veishnava women have a perpendicular red mark with a horizontal white mark between the eyes.

The worshipers of Shiva have three horizontal lines on the forehead. In the early morning these are made of *vibhuti,* or sacred ashes, which are prepared with special ceremonies and the utterance of *mantrams,* or prayers. After bathing, the sacred ashes are replaced by sandal-paste, or *shandanam.* Very often a circular white spot, as mentioned before, takes the place of the three lines. This circular spot is called *pottu.* Shiva women have a crim-

BLACKSMITHS.

(From a native drawing.)

See page 32.

son *pottu* made of turmeric and lime-juice. Andis or Sheiva ascetics smear the whole body with these sacred ashes. It is an essential part of the religious duty of every Hindu to inscribe these sectarian marks on his person each day (a bag or small box of the material being kept in every house for the purpose), just as it is incumbent on every convert from Hinduism, as one of his first duties on embracing the Christian faith, to remove these symbols of heathenism.

The clothing of the Hindus is singularly graceful, becoming, and suited to the country. The men wear two snow-white cloths, each from two to ten yards in length, the one "an upper cloth" and the other a "lower cloth." The former is thrown over the shoulders, somewhat like a Roman toga, and covers the body with the exception of the head and arms; the latter, which consists of a single piece, is wound round the waist, and falls below the knees more or less to the ground. There are no pins, buttons, or strings, but it is fastened by simply folding one part within the other. Sometimes, if sufficiently long, one end of this cloth is passed between the legs from behind, and arranged in folds in front. Many, however, among the educated classes now wear made-up tunics, while others wear loose and tight trousers, like the Mohammedans, the latter fastening them on the left side, and the former on the right. The turban or headdress consists of a long, narrow piece of cloth wound round the head, its shape and color being adapted to the taste of the wearer. Many may be seen in the streets without any head-covering at all, but no one is admitted into European or other respectable society without a headdress. Stockings are seldom or never seen. The wearing of shoes is optional; many go without them, but sandals or native slippers peaked and turned up at the toes, and turned down at the heels, are usually worn outside but never inside the house. Natives of all castes take off their shoes and retain their turbans when visiting others, or when receiving visitors themselves. Among the educated classes it is becoming customary to wear boots, and sometimes even patent-leather ones. Finger rings, ear rings, and toe rings are also worn by the men.

All Brahmins, as well as the other "twice-born" castes, wear a thread, called the sacred thread (*punul*), which hangs from the left shoulder across to the right side. This they put on between the ages of eight and fifteen. It consists of three thick twists of cotton, each formed of several smaller threads. The three threads are separate from one another, and on the marriage of a Brahmin the three threads are increased to nine. It is renewed every year. Religious Brahmins wear round the neck a rosary of hard nuts of certain trees, which is used in reciting the appointed prayers. Sivites wear a rosary of Rudraksham nuts; Vishnuvites, a rosary made of the nuts of the tulsi tree.

The dress of the women consists of one piece of

cloth from six to twenty yards in length, and one or two yards in width, one end of which, being gathered in folds, is held to the left side, while the other end is wound round the waist and brought up over the right shoulder and down to the left side, where it is tucked in so as to fall down the front in folds. This cloth is generally colored and embroidered, and sometimes of silk. Petticoats are now worn by some women. Widows are allowed to wear only a white cloth. In addition to the cloth, a short, tight-fitting jacket with short sleeves is worn. The women wear no headdress, but a single fold of cloth is drawn up over the head.

All women are passionately fond of jewelry, which they wear on their arms, necks, and fingers, in their ears and noses, round their ankles, between their toes, and in their hair. The ornaments on the feet are invariably of silver. The most important ornament worn by married Hindu women is the *talee*. It answers to the wedding-ring among the English, and consists of one or more small gold jewels on a twisted thread. This is fastened round the neck of the bride by the bridegroom at the time of marriage, and is never removed except in case of widowhood. Brahmin women wear the cloth wound round the waist in the usual manner, but with five folds in front and behind, like the men. Occasionally the end which hangs down behind is brought forward between the legs and fastened in front, leaving the legs behind uncovered. All women smear their faces and the uncovered portions of their bodies with a yellow solution of saffron and water, which is supposed to make them "fair." They also paint the border of the eyelashes with a solution of oil and lamp-black, and redden their finger nails with a dye of henna leaves. Hindu women usually have the feet uncovered.

The dress of Mohammedan men usually consists of a pair of drawers, a long, flowing robe, gathered together into folds just below the chest, and the folds sewed together, a small cap on the head covered with a turban, a handkerchief, and shoes. Mohammedan women have a long, flowing robe, a bodice, a petticoat, shoes on the feet, and the usual full complement of jewels.

The wearing of the hair long, tied up in a knot at the back of the head, still frequently seen, was the original Tamil custom. The mode now in general use, however, among all respectable classes is to shave off all the hair of the head, leaving only a small tuft at the back. The inhabitants of the west coast wear the tuft at the front of the head over the forehead. A caste of bankers in Tinnevelly and Madura shave the head completely, like the Mohammedans. When a Hindu loses his father or mother, he shaves off his tuft of hair, and also his mustache, as a sign of mourning. The Hindus wear only the mustache on the face, and sometimes side whiskers, but seldom or never wear a full beard. The wearing of a beard generally indicates some vow. The women have long, black, glossy hair. which they tie up in a knot at the back of the head; but some castes place it at the side. The young girls plait their hair in braids hanging down behind, much in the same fashion as American girls; but without the red and blue ribbons at the end. Sweet-smelling flowers are not infrequently tastefully placed in the hair, which have a very pleasing effect.

When a Hindu visits a European gentleman, the first thing he does is to take off his shoes, which he leaves outside in the veranda of the house, but keeps on his turban. He then approaches and makes a *salaam*, by raising his right hand to his forehead and letting it drop again to his side. Hand-shaking is now becoming common among the educated and enlightened. After this he presents you with two or more limes or lemons as a peace-offering, which you must receive with your right hand. You then request him to be seated, which he does; either sitting crosslegged on the floor, or else sitting on a chair. You then inquire about his welfare, avoiding all reference to his wife, to which he usually replies by saying that by "your honor's favor, and the grace of the Almighty," he is well.

The conversation now proceeds, during which he is studiously polite, striving not to offend you in any way, but to return such answers as he thinks will please you. When the interview has lasted sufficiently long, you tell him that he may go. No

Hindu will go until he is told to leave. If you wish to see him again, you say, "Go, and come again." Otherwise you simply say, "Go." This would not be at all an inconvenient custom to introduce among the Americans, where some persons unnecessarily occupy a large portion of one's time! Leaving the room, after having made a salaam, he puts on his shoes, and proceeds on his way. If he meets a respectable native gentleman of his own standing in society, or of a superior position, he salutes him by joining the two palms of his hands together, raising them to the level of his forehead, and letting them drop again. Brahmins generally salute the members of their own caste, and receive the salutations of others. If he sees a European official, or a gentleman of high social position, driving past, he either stands at the roadside, takes off his shoes, and salutes him with a low, reverential bow, or he makes an ordinary salaam in passing. He never salutes or takes any notice of a female. If he passes a temple by the roadside, it is not improbable that he will stop, take off his shoes, put the two palms of his hands together, mutter a few prayers, and then, putting on his shoes, pass on. Sometimes he may be seen prostrating himself before the idol. When a Hindu enters the presence of his spiritual teacher, he prostrates himself before him, and holds his feet.

The houses of the Hindus are mostly one story in height, though some are two-storied. They are built of clay bricks dried in the sun, and whitewashed with *chunam*, a kind of lime. They have an open veranda towards the street. The door is placed in the middle. Entering this door, you come into a small room with a raised *pial*, or alcove, on each side. Here the owner receives his guests. Passing on, you come to an open court, paved, but not roofed. The rooms are built round this court, and open into it. They are mostly small and dark, and fitted with wooden bars. One room is set apart for the use of the females, and the others for the other members of the family, as well as for various domestic purposes, such as cooking food, eating, storing grain, etc. The household gods (*lares* and *penates*) are usually kept in the kitchen, and worship is paid to them before eating. In respectable houses a special room is set apart for this purpose, where anyone who wishes may retire for worship, in addition to visiting the public temples. There are no tables or chairs, but a low bedstead, called a *charpoi*, without mattress, a box for keeping clothes and jewels, a rush mat, and a few earthen and metal pots, constitute all the furniture.

Some of the educated and wealthier classes now have chairs, tables, couches, pictures, lamps, etc., but this is not the general custom. In large houses there is often a second smaller court and a small garden. A well is dug in the garden for convenience. The ceiling, rafters, and beams are of teak or palmyra wood, and the roof is covered with tiles.

The dwellings of the poorest natives consist of four mud walls, with bamboo rafters covered with grass or palm-leaf thatch. Cows, buffaloes, and fowls are freely admitted inside an ordinary Hindu house, and may even be seen entering at the front door. A Hindu of the higher and middle classes, on rising in the morning, generally goes to a neighboring tank (lake), where he cleans his teeth, performs his sacred ablutions, inscribes sectarian marks on his forehead, arms, and breasts, visits the temple, and returns home to take a small repast before entering on the duties of the day.

The Hindus usually have but two meals a day —one at twelve o'clock, and the other at night, when the day's work is over, and before retiring to rest. "Pepper water," a kind of soup without meat, and a little of the cold rice left over from the previous night, or else a rice cake, called *hoppah*, and coffee or tea, are now frequently partaken of before the noon-day meal, on rising in the morning. The laboring classes, who go to their work early and remain out during the day, take their first meal in the early morning instead of at noon. The principal food of the country is curry and rice. Curry is a kind of powder made of pepper, salt, turmeric, ginger, tamarinds, onions, cocoanut juice, garlic, saffron, etc., mixed so as to suit the taste of the individual. The ingredients are ground on a smooth flat stone with a stone roller. This is added to the fish, fowl, piece of mutton, or vegetable, which is boiled in an earthen vessel. The rice is also boiled in water in an earthen vessel. The repast is now ready.

There are no tables, chairs, knives, forks, or spoons. The individual sits crosslegged on the ground. A plantain leaf, sometimes several fig leaves sewn together, form the plate. The curry and rice is placed on this. It is customary for the female members of the house to cook the food. When it is ready, it is brought to the male members and set before them. The fingers are used in eating. Some of the curry and rice is taken, rolled up into a sort of ball, and thrown into the mouth. The females never eat with the males. The male members eat first, and when they have finished and are satisfied, the females, who meanwhile have been attending on them, eat the remainder from the same leaf plate. Water, which is drunk out of a brass vessel, is the common drink; but some among the educated classes have, unfortunately, imbibed a taste for English wines and spirits, while others of the poorer classes drink *tadi*, or toddy, the fermented juice of the palmyra tree, or *arrack*, a country spirit distilled from toddy or *jaggery* (raw sugar).

Ragi is the grain chiefly eaten by the laboring classes. It is cheaper than rice, and more sustaining for those who have to undergo bodily exertion. *Ghee* (clarified butter), butter-milk, and curds are used by all classes. Green vegetables are used in curries, and ripe fruits are eaten raw when in season, such as plantains, mangoes, custard-apple, jack-fruit, melons, cocoanut, etc. Sweetmeats are largely partaken of, principally made of sugar, butter, and flour. Some of these foods are healthful as well as palatable, but many of their dishes, to a Western taste, would be intolerable. It is strange how man abuses, by cooking, mixing, fermenting, and distilling, God's wondrous gifts.

CHAPTER V.

MANNERS AND CUSTOMS—CONTINUED.

Amusements—Hindu Jugglers—Birth, Marriage, Death, and Funeral Ceremonies—Joint Family System—Division of Family Property—Adoption.

THE Hindus, like most people, are not over-fond of work, and delight in amusements and pastimes of all descriptions. The more noise and display the better they appreciate a thing. One of their amusements is telling and listening to wonderful stories about their gods and heroes. Other amusements are card playing and chess. Witnessing feats of jugglery and legerdemain is another favorite pastime. The Indian jugglers are, many of them, wonderfully clever, and their performances are all the more astounding from the fact that they are stark naked, with the exception of a small piece of cloth round their waists and a turban on their heads. There is no stage erection, no curtains, tables, etc., only the bare ground before you and the open sky above.

One of their tricks is called the "mango-tree trick." A quantity of earth is taken and placed on the ground before you, in which the seed of a mango tree is imbedded. It is covered over with a cloth, and in a short time a movement takes place. The cloth is uncovered, and you see a small tree growing with leaves, etc.

Another common performance is the "basket trick." An open basket of medium size is taken and shown to you. It is placed on the ground before you, and a girl or young woman doubled up and corded all over is placed in it. The basket is then covered with a lid and a cloth about the size of a sheet put over it. A man takes a sword and stabs the basket all round. A cry is heard, as if the girl had been injured, but the man jumps on the lid, and the basket is empty. There is no appearance of the girl, only the cord with which she was fastened is to be found. Snake charming is also a favorite amusement.

In the evenings *nautches*, or performances of dancing women, are held. They answer much the same purpose as theaters among Europeans. The *nautch* girls are not infrequently good-looking, but they are low, abandoned characters. Resplendent with jewels, they advance before the audience and dance gracefully, but with little variety, to the accompaniment of native music. They throw the body into all kinds of positions, and their arms move in unison with their feet; but the full meaning of their motions and gestures is known only to the initiated. Sometimes cotton ropes are suspended, and the *nautch* girls, moving in and out among

(From a native drawing.)

SAWYERS.

See page 32.

themselves, holding the rope in one hand and a stick in the other, with which they beat the stick of the opposite party, weave the ropes into all kinds of mathematical figures. The natives sit for hours watching a performance of this kind. If a native gentleman gives an entertainment to Europeans, it invariably winds up with a *nautch*.

The birth of a child in a Hindu family is an event of great importance. If it is a son that is born, the occasion is one of great rejoicing. If it is a girl, there is little joy expressed, because sons only can perform the funeral ceremonies of the father, on which his happiness in the future world depends, and also on account of the great expense necessarily attending a daughter's marriage. When a child is born, a Brahmin priest is summoned, who casts its horoscope, announcing the planet under which it is born, and detailing the principal circumstances of its future history. This horoscope is carefully treasured, and is consulted on all important occasions.

When the child is a few days old, the ceremony of naming it takes place. A priest is summoned, the parents sit on the ground, and the priest gives the father a plate of raw rice, on which he inscribes the name of the child and the planet under which it was born. This name is thrice pronounced; the ceremony then terminates with an offering to the household gods and a fee and dinner to the priest and as many invited guests as the father's means will permit. It is important to invite as many as have any claim to be present, as the omission of anyone might entail his enmity in the future. When a father hesitates between several names, he writes them down, places a lighted lamp before each, and chooses the one before which the lamp burns the longest. Hindus name their children generally after some god or goddess, as Krishna, Rama, Narayana, Parvati, etc. Occasionally a name descriptive of personal excellence is given, as Gnana-pragasam (shining wisdom), Deva-dass (servant of God), Masillamaui (faultless pearl), etc. Before this name they place their village name, and after it their caste title.

Colonel Sleeman, in his "Rambles and Recollections of an Indian Official," says:—

"Marriage is a sacred duty among the Hindus, a duty which every parent must perform for his children. It fills their imagination from infancy to age. A family with a marriageable daughter unmarried is considered to be under the displeasure of the gods, and no member of the male sex considers himself respectable until he is married. Nothing strikes the Hindus so strangely as the utter indifference of old bachelors among the English to their sad and deplorable condition.

"Very large sums of money are spent in marriage feasts and ceremonies. Nothing is more common than to see an individual in the humblest rank spending all that he has, or can borrow, in the marriage of one of many daughters, and trusting to Providence for the means wherewith to marry the others. The reason for this appears to be that under the old despotic government men could never feel secure of being permitted freely to enjoy their property. Even a man's right to the exclusive possession of his wife was not considered altogether secure under the mere sanction of religion. He, therefore, strengthened his security by an outlay in feeding the family tribe and neighborhood during the marriage ceremony, which invested his wife with a certain tangible value. The family tribe and circle having received the purchase money, as it were, felt bound to secure to him the "commodity" purchased. The increased feeling of security to person and property under the British rule will doubtless cause this custom gradually to decline."

A Hindu marriage is, as will easily be seen, an expensive affair, and usually lasts from seven to ten days. There is no courtship. The marriage contract is arranged by the parents, and the boy and girl, who are usually married at six and eight years respectively, are neither consulted nor given any opportunity of seeing each other before the ceremony takes place. There are two separate ceremonies in a Hindu marriage. The first is, properly speaking, the betrothal, and the second, which takes place when the girl has attained the age of twelve or thirteen, is the real marriage. Nevertheless, if the husband dies before the second ceremony takes place, the girl becomes a widow for life.

Marriage customs vary with different castes, but in most of the marriages the bride and bridegroom walk round an altar, on which a fire burns, three times, and then prostrate themselves in honor of the deity. After this the girl touches fire and water, in token of her willingness to perform household duties. The husband and wife then eat together for the first and only time in their lives. These ceremonies being over, general conversation ensues among the guests, or some recitations are made by any learned Brahmins who may happen to be present.

After this betrothal, or first marriage, is over, the girl returns to her parents' house and remains with them until the age of twelve or thirteen. She is then taken to her father-in-law's house, and lives there with her husband. Even though there may be many married sons in the house, they all live together until the father dies, when the eldest son takes his place, and so on. In this way separate families are formed, the grown-up sons with their wives and children living in their father's house and subject to his control, the married daughters alone going to their father-in-law's house, where they are often treated with great harshness by their mother-in-law. The chief qualities sought for in a bride are not mental or moral ones, but she is commended because she is moon-faced of graceful figure, sweet speech, and can cook well. The highest praise that can be bestowed on a bride is that she can cook well.

If no sons are borne by the wife, the husband is at liberty to take a second wife, but he must also maintain the first wife. The following account has been given by a Mohammedan gentleman with reference to the marriage customs of the Mohammedans :—

"The priest, who sits next to the bridegroom, inquires who will be the witnesses of the marriage. This being settled, he asks the bridegroom thrice if he accepts the bride as his wife, and also asks the father or guardian whether he gives her away. The bride is all this time, with other ladies, in a separate room. Then the priest registers the names of the party and witnesses, the date of the marriage, and the dowry. This being done, he recites some passages from Mohammedan Scriptures, and blesses the couple, raising his hands toward heaven. When all this is done, the bridegroom removes his veil and flowers from his face, which he has had on for nearly six hours. He gets up from his seat and salutes the people around him, and not he but his father is congratulated by them all in return. He then receives a cup of milk to drink. Now comes the last and most interesting part of the ceremony. He is asked to go and visit the ladies who are with the bride. When he reaches the door, younger relatives of the bride half open it, and ask a toll from him for admission to the room. He has to give them something. When they have received their toll, they close the door on him, and all retire except the bride. Then a signal is made to him to enter the room. He finds there the bride, all alone, covered with a veil which is tied around her head. He removes the veil, puts an ornament on her person, and gives her some sweetmeat which is at hand to eat. Thus the bride is first seen by her husband after her marriage, and, most probably, they then see each other for the first time in their lives."

After giving an idea of the miseries of Mohammedan women, he says:—

"The ideas of morality and decency among Mohammedans are so strict that a respectable Mohammedan husband would not think of consulting a doctor on his wife's illness. He would rather let her die than allow her face to be seen by a gentleman! She would not think of protesting against it, as she is ground down by custom, and has no individuality. In extreme cases of illness the most scrupulous husband relaxes his standard of decency somewhat. He allows his wife to be placed behind a curtain, and lets her put out her hand, for the doctor to feel her pulse. Even then his sense of the sacredness and inviolableness of her person is so high that he would not allow the doctor to touch her bare hand, but would persist in putting a thin piece of muslin over her hand and wrist. He would also blush ten times before he allowed his wife to put her tongue through a slit in the curtain for the doctor to see it."

The funeral ceremonies of different castes vary somewhat in details, but the following is the general procedure among the more respectable classes: When a man is dying he is placed on kusha grass; this is a kind of bean straw, and is supposed to have the efficacy of destroying sin. The relatives then pour into his mouth drops of milk, and call out their own names, so that they may be remembered in the future world. When the man is dead, the eldest son, assisted by the other relatives, washes the deceased's head and anoints it with oil. The dead body is then wrapped in a new cloth—if a man, in a white one; if a woman, in a red one—and placed on a bier in a half-sitting posture. Ground rice and betel are placed in his mouth. The women, with hair disheveled, then weep and mourn, and beat their breasts. Hired mourners are called in to keep up the lamentation when the real mourners are exhausted.

This being over, the body is carried out, the eldest son leading the way with fire in a vessel. and music follows behind. The male relatives alone follow the body, the females remaining in the house. If a person of distinction dies, cloths are placed on the ground over which the procession passes, the cloths being repeatedly taken up and placed before it. When the dead body has arrived at the burning-place, it is placed, with the head towards the north, on the funeral pyre, which has in the meantime been prepared. The eldest son then walks three times round the pyre with a torch in his hand and a pot of water on his shoulder. After this he applies the torch to the wood—in the direction of the head if the deceased is a male, but in the direction of the feet if a female. At the same time he lets the pot drop from his shoulder, so that it breaks and the water falls on the ground. He then bathes in water close by, and returns home without looking round, so that the deceased's sin may not fall on his head. The remaining ceremonies are performed by corpse burners hired for the purpose.

The widow, if there is one, remains under the protection of the eldest son, who in all respects assumes the father's place as the head of the family. The widow either lives upon the property left by her husband, or when she has children is supported by them. If there is neither property nor children, her nearest relative supports her. Failing everything, she will go to a stranger's house and engage in domestic duties, by which she will maintain herself.

Cremation is practiced by the Hindus with few exceptions. Only devotees and ascetics of the highest rank, and *mahunts*, or heads of monasteries, who are considered specially holy, are buried. The Mohammedans always bury. After a death, the relatives of the deceased are ceremonially unclean for ten days, and, as already stated, shave off in token of mourning the *kudumi*, or tuft of hair on their heads, and also the mustache.

The peculiarity of Hindu social life is the joint family system, according to which all live in subordination to the elected head, who is, generally speaking, the oldest male. In case of unfitness another will be elected. In this country each married couple forms a unit of society, capable of thinking and acting for themselves. But in India it is not so. There, when a child is born into the world, he forms part of a great household, consisting not only of his parents, but also of many others—all under the headship of some aged member. They may live in one house or in several, but they still form one organization.

In this great household the parents have no independent control over their own children, nor are the children themselves ever consulted, but everything is done with the consent of the elders, and in strict accordance with the family traditions, whether they be right or wrong. Property is also held conjointly. When a division takes place, as on the death of a father, each inherits only his share. Where, on the death of a father, a family of brothers is managed by the eldest, he is treated by the rest with respect, as if he were their father. The adoption of children is allowed, in which case they share equally with the children of the fathers and mothers who adopt them.

The ceremony of adoption is simple. The person who wishes to adopt summons his relatives, and, while the child is standing in a large copper dish, addresses them thus: "We inform you that, having no child, we wish to adopt this one. We choose him for our child in this wise, that our goods shall belong to him henceforth as if he were actually born of us. He has now nothing to hope for from his own father. In token whereof we are now going to drink saffron water, if you consent." Those present having consented by shaking their heads, the adopting parties wash the child's feet in saffron water from a vase, and drink part of what remains. The ceremony is now complete, and is recorded in a deed testified by witnesses. If the adopting father and mother subsequently have natural children, they are subordinate to the adopted, inasmuch as the law makes no difference between the adopted and real child.

CHAPTER VI.

RELIGION AND WORSHIP.

Demon Worship—Tutelar Village Deities—The Hindu Triad: Brahma, Vishnu, Shiva—Tree Worship—Serpent Worship.

THE Hindu is a religious person. His ideas of God and of his worship are peculiar to himself, but he is, nevertheless, intensely in earnest. To a Hindu his every act has a religious meaning entering into the very fibers and threadlets of his life. It is the Alpha and Omega, the beginning and end of his existence. There is no fast or feast, no event of joy or sorrow in his life, but whatever he does he does it to the glory of his god. To the Hindu the Deity is literally omnipresent. A belief in the divine presence fills his whole life.

The modern Hindu religion is of a composit nature. The people are no longer sharply divided into civilized Aryans and rude non-Aryans, but have arranged themselves into graduated castes of a great mixed population. Their religious and family life is a compromise between Aryan spiritual conceptions and non-Aryan superstitions—a commingling of non-Aryan darkness with Aryan light. The pantheon of worship includes one set of deities quite aboriginal, and another which they have derived from the Brahminical system. Modern Hinduism is no more the old Vedic religion than the great mass of the people of India are pure Aryans. The mixed Hindu religion of South India may be thus classified.

1. *Demon Worship.*—They hold that demons may have originated in many ways, but, generally speaking, they are the disembodied spirits of human beings. The majority are supposed to inhabit trees, but others wander to and fro. All misfortunes in business, all sickness of children, and all disease among cattle, are supposed to be caused by them. The unseen world is said to be hostile to man; and the good-will of the demons is to be gained by incantations and sacrifices, which require the shedding of animal blood. The demons are of three kinds: (1) The *peys*, which take possession of men; (2) the *boothams*, which haunt the places where dead bodies are burned or buried; (3) the *pishauch*, which is the most active and troublesome of all the demons.

The devil temples are called *peycous*. They consist of a small pyramidal erection of earth covered with streaks of whitewash and red paint, with a smaller heap having a flat surface, which forms the altar. There is no special priestly class connected with devil worship; any, even the women, may act as priests or devil dancers, provided they

WEAVERS.

(*From a native drawing.*)

See page 34.

are duly inspired by the demon who is invoked. At nights the demon is supposed to wander about, alluring people from their houses in order to kill them. Demons are supposed to call only three times, and hence calls at night are never responded to until the fourth time. Many children are dedicated to and named after demons, in order to escape infantile diseases. Sometimes the eldest son is named after the demon worshiped by the father's family, and the eldest daughter after that of the mother's family. Demon worship is most common among the Shanars, or palm cultivators, of Tinnevelly, in Travancore, Malabar, and South Canara, where the population has been the least disturbed by Brahminical influence.

2. *Grama-devatas, or Tutelar Village Deities.*—Every village contains one temple dedicated to its tutelar deity. Strange to say, all the village deities, with one exception, who is called Ayenaur, are females, and have the name *ammah* (mother) attached to them. They are supposed to protect the village from sickness and disaster. The principal are Mariyammah and Pidari. Mariyammah is the goddess of smallpox and measles. When a person is attacked with smallpox, the goddess is supposed to take possession of him, and, rather than offend her, the patient is often allowed to die without any remedies being tried. A non-Brahmin priest, called a *pujari*, officiates at these temples. He anoints the deity—which is represented by a

black stone—daily with oil, and offers sacrifices, the commonest of which are cocoanuts, which he breaks in front of the idol. Cocks, goats, and sheep are also sacrificed. Annual festivals lasting several days are also celebrated in honor of each goddess of the various villages. In their temples are to be found other images, most commonly Pillaiyar, the belly-god. When Ayenaur, the male tutelar deity, is worshiped, propitiatory offerings are made in fulfillment of vows by presenting clay images of horses, on which the god is supposed to take occasional nightly rides. In addition to the village deities other smaller deites are worshiped in the shape of a stone or a lump of clay marked with red or black in secluded spots or under a tree without any temple.

3. *The Devas or Secondary Gods.*—These are said to be three hundred and thirty thousand in number, and include the *rishis* (sages) and the regents of the eight cardinal points of the earth, such as Indra, Agni, Varuna, etc. These have no temple, and are little worshiped.

4. *The Trimurthi: Brahma, Vishnu, and Shiva.*—The word "*trimurthi*" means "three forms." The majority of the people regard one or the other as the supreme being, though some consider them as a tri-unity—three in one. These are the chief objects of worship in South India.. *Brahma*, though the highest in rank and dignity, has no temple erected to his honor and no national worship paid

to him, except the honor paid to the Brahmins, who are regarded as his offspring. He is said to write in every man's forehead his destiny—how long he is to live and what is to happen to him. He is also said to be the author of the Vedas, which he gave to the *rishi* (sage) Vedavyasa to promulgate in the world. His wife is Saraswati, the goddess of learning.

The great bulk of the population worship Shiva. Though he is represented in the arts as of gigantic size, riding on a bull, with bloodshot eyes and serpents hanging like jewels from his ears, yet he has no separate image. The outward representation of Shiva is always the *lingam.* The *lingam* is a small black stone. This is carried about by his disciples either in a silver box round the neck or fastened to the arm. It is called *jangaman*, or "movable," in contradistinction to the *lingam* of the temples, which is called *stauvaram*, or stable. The heaven of Shiva is called Keilasa, and his vehicle, as already stated, is a bull, which is always found in front of his temples. His wife is Parvati, and his two sons Vigneshvara (remover of obstacles), and Subramanian (diamond-like). The former is known under various names, meaning, son, great lord, lord of hosts. He is usually represented with an elephant's head and trunk, and a big stomach, and hence is called the "belly-god" by Europeans. His image is found everywhere by the roadside and under trees. Many small pagodas, or temples, are also erected in his honor, in which he is daily worshiped with offerings.

Vishnu is worshiped in numerous pagodas by large numbers, who regard him as the supreme being. He is said to assume ten incarnations; that is, he appears to men in different forms of material objects ten times; for instance, in the form of a fish, a tortoise, a boar, a lion, a dwarf, as a man named Parasrama, as a king called Rama, as Krishna, and in the plurality incarnation, in which he was incarnate in his twelve disciples, called *alwars*. His last incarnation is yet to come. His nine completed incarnations and the tenth expected one are famous in Hindu religion. On these occasions he appeared to deliver oracles, to destroy giants, and to relieve the world from the woes under which it groaned. His wife's name is Lutchmi, the goddess of beauty and fortune, and his son's name Kama, the Indian cupid, or god of love. As the *lingam* and the *yony* are the symbolic representations of Shiva and his wife Parvati, so the *salagram*, a petrified ammonite found on the banks of the Gandakee, and the tulsi plant, are the symbols of Vishnu and his wife Latchmi. Again, what the bull is to Shiva that the monkeys are to Vishnu. Swarms of these infest the neighborhood of his temples, where they are kept and fed as the representatives of Hanuman, the monkey-god who was associated with Rama. The living monkey is considered in some sense to be divine, and no native will kill a monkey, even when it commits depredation in the fields. In many towns and villages may be seen a large stone image four or five feet high, in the shape of a monkey, which is painted red, with staring eyes and erect tail, and which is worshiped by all classes.

Tree worship is also found in India. Trees, on account of their beauty and utility, are not only regarded as fit abodes of the gods, but as suitable objects of worship in themselves. This worship is to be found in almost all countries. The Assyrians, Greeks, Romans, and Druids had their sacred groves. In South India, also, the reverence paid to single trees or sacred groves is very prevalent. Many Brahmins like to have the sacred tulsi tree growing in front of their houses, and it is frequently found in front of temples. The *peepul*, or fig tree, is also invested with sanctity; and young married couples may be seen walking round it with folded hands many times, in order to gain the blessing of offspring.

The serpent, on account of the celerity and gracefulness of its movements and its exceptional powers of destruction, is an object of worship. The snake is associated with other deities, and is represented in the carved idols placed in temples. Carved representations of the cobra, sometimes a single one semi-erect with expanded hood, and sometimes two snakes intertwined, are frequently to be seen set up in groves by the roadside or under the sacred

6

peepul tree. Offerings are daily made at these shrines, and every woman who desires to have off-spring brings offerings of milk, *ghee* (clarified butter), eggs, or flowers. *Naga* (snake) stones are usually in sets of three. The first represents a seven-headed cobra. The second is a female, the lower portion of whose body is that of a snake. The third represents two serpents entwined, the children of the former. Naga stones, when properly erected, are on a stone platform facing the east, and under the shadow of two peepul trees. They are most numerous near Jain temples. Living snakes are also worshiped. An old woman had an only son, a *sepoy*, who was ordered to Burmah. He left his mother five rupees a month out of his pay. She found a cobra in an ant hill, and made offerings of milk and eggs to it regularly, praying that her son might soon return. One day she raised her clasped hands to her head in the attitude of prayer, but, coming too near the snake, it became frightened and bit her. She died within two hours. Serpent or naga worship is generally considered to have been introduced from the North.

CHAPTER VII.

RELIGION AND WORSHIP—CONTINUED.

Temples — Mode of Worship — Festivals — Pilgrimages— Omens and Superstitions—Buddhism—Fear the Predominant Feeling in Worship.

FOR the worship of the gods of the Hindu pantheon temples abound all over the country. The temples of South India are much larger than those of North India, and are probably the largest in the world. It is considered impious to live in a street without a temple. Not only in towns and villages, but on the tops of hills, in deserted places, by the roadside, by tanks and rivers, temples are to be found. The largest temples of South India are those at Srirangam, Chidambram, Madura, Tanjore, Trivellore, Tripati, and Conjeveram. That at Srirangam, near Trichinopoly, is nearly four miles in circumference, and is surrounded by seven walls. All the large temples are surrounded by high walls, and have massive towers, called *gopurams*, covered from top to bottom with figures, over the four entrances. Almost all the temples have a tank attached to them, and there are also pillared halls for pilgrims. Inside the temples are idols of gold or silver, iron or brass, and sometimes only of clay. These idols are anointed every morning and evening with melted butter or milk. The anointing is accompanied with ceremonies and prayers. The idea is that after these prayers and ceremonies the god takes possession of the idol, which until then was only an image. The idol is then covered with garlands of flowers, or flowers are strewed in front of it. Not only Brahmins, but even Sudra priests, officiate at some of the temples.

The Hindus of South India have no fixed hours for worship, nor have they any common worship, like Christians. Each one worships by himself and for himself. He repairs to the temple with his offering, and makes his way to the inner sanctuary, where the god is placed in a niche with an oil lamp burning by its side. He presents his offering, consisting of cocoanuts, fruit, or flowers. He stands before the image with folded hands in adoration, muttering its name several times, or walks round and round the idol doing the same thing. Prayer in the Christian sense is unknown. He makes no confession of sin, asks for no forgiveness, nor does he desire purity and holiness. He simply prays for riches and prosperity, asks to be delivered from some calamity, and requests the god to give him a son, and not a daughter, on account of the expense which the latter entails. His devotions are now over, and, having paid his fee to the officiating

A POTTER.

From a native drawing.)

See page 36.

priest, he goes his way; but before doing so has three broad streaks either horizontally or perpendicularly marked on his forehead. These are worn throughout the day, and testify to the fact that he has worshiped in the temple, and is to be considered as a religious person.

Many educated Hindus in the present day worship no idols and observe no ceremonies. They merely keep pictures of Rama, Krishna, or Sarasvati in their houses. Those who are more devout light camphor in the evening in front of these pictures, and decorate them with garlands of flowers, repeating the names of the god. Besides this daily worship there are special festivals connected with certain temples, especially those at Conjeveram, Tripati, Trivellore, Tirutani, Tirunamalli, Ramisweram, and Srirangam. These festivals last for several days, and people throng to them in thousands from all parts. The principal god is carried round the chief streets of the town on large cars fifty feet high, built like one of the *gopurams*, or towers, covered with grotesque figures and carvings of the gods. The idol cars move on solid wheels without spokes; stout ropes are attached in front, and hundreds of people pull at them. They must be pulled by men, and not animals, and the progress is very slow.

These festivals, associated as they are with religious observances, have a wonderful fascination for the Hindu. They are largely kept up by the women, who look forward to them as a welcome respite from the imprisonment of their homes. The farmer also marks the progress of time by means of these festivals. All the leading events in his otherwise uneventful life are associated with them. A Hindu will suspend all business for ten days or a fortnight in order that he and all the members of his family, gaily dressed in holiday attire, may attend one of them, and there engage in sports, rejoicings, and devotions connected with some old historical event of national interest. These festivals have all the appearance of a fair. Much buying and selling is done, and there are all kinds of amusements both for the young and the old. Devotees of all kinds may be seen. Some are almost naked and covered with ashes. Others are dressed in a yellow robe, unwashed and unkempt, with a begging pot, consisting of a dried gourd, in the hand. Others, again, go about singing songs in the street to the accompaniment of music played on a one-stringed instrument like a guitar, in order to excite the charity of the bystanders. Men may be seen with iron spikes driven through their cheeks, or carrying an iron cage round their necks, in fulfillment of some vow.

Messengers are sent all over the country by the managers of all the large temples, to give notice of these festivals and the time of their occurrence. That at Conjeveram takes place in the month of May, and lasts ten days. It is attended by immense crowds of people from all parts. Besides the festivals connected with certain temples, there are certain feasts which occur once a year, and which are observed by all the people all over the country. The principal of these is Pongal, which takes place in the Hindu month of Tai, *i. e.*, about the middle of January. It lasts three days, and is occupied with rejoicings and the visitation of friends. Every day of the previous month, the month of December, has been unlucky, and every day of the succeeding month is lucky. Hence the rejoicings.

During the month of December, in order to ward off evil, women draw white lines with flour before the door of their houses. Upon these they place balls of cow manure, each bearing a citron blossom. The balls are picked up each day and preserved. On the last day of the month (December) they are gathered together by the women, put in a basket, and to the accompaniment of music, thrown away in some waste place. On the first day near relatives are feasted and entertained; the second day is the great day of visitation. Rice and milk are boiled in the open air. When it begins to simmer, all present cry *pongal*, signifying boiling. They salute each other by saying, "Has the milk boiled?" The answer given is, "It has boiled." On the third day the cows are sprinkled with a mixture of saffron and water, their horns painted, decorated with garlands, and are then turned out to graze wherever they like without a keeper.

Another important feast is the Telugu and Tamil New Year. The Telugu New Year falls about the end of March, and the Tamil New Year the middle of April. On these occasions each person anoints his body with oil, and washes with warm water in the morning. In the evening the family priest reads out from the new almanac what is to happen during the year. There are also fireworks, etc. Another feast is Pillaiyar Chavuti, when Pillaiyar, the son of Shiva, is worshiped as the remover of difficulties from all undertakings. Clay images of the god are made, consecrated, duly worshiped, and then thrown into the river or tank. The Ayudha or Sarasvati feast is also an important one. It falls generally in October. On this occasion each worships the tools or implements by which he gains his livelihood. The farmer worships his plow, the mason his trowel, the clerk his paper and pen, the scholar his books, and the women their rice pounders, etc. The Brahmins worship Sarasvati, the goddess of learning, and the upper classes of Hindu society make offerings of rice, fruit, flowers, and cloths, to their ancestors. The Depavali, or feast of lights, is another important festival. It falls usually at the end of October or the beginning of November. On this occasion at sunset small open earthen vessels containing oil and a wick lapping over the edge are put in front of every house; the humblest hut has at least one. They are also placed on the tops of hills, in the clefts of trees, and in other prominent positions. The wicks are lit in all directions, so that there is a general illumination, and the effect as the darkness increases is very pretty. Guns are fired, and crackers and fireworks displayed. This feast is probably a relic of old fire worship.

Pilgrimages to sacred shrines are often undertaken, and hundreds of Hindus are continually wandering over the country on pilgrimages. In various parts of South India groups of pilgrims may be seen in the streets, crying out, "Govinda," "Govinda," "Rama," "Rama." The women, both old and young, have their heads shaved quite bald, their hair having been presented to the shrine of the gods at Tripati. Pilgrims from the north may also be seen, each carrying two baskets united by a bamboo and borne on the shoulders. Each basket contains numerous small phials filled with holy water from the Ganges, or some other sacred stream, and hermetically sealed. When all his wanderings have ceased, these are either distributed by the pilgrim among those who have contributed towards his expenses, or else poured out as a libation on the occasion of the consecration of a temple or an image. The proper way of performing a pilgrimage is to walk the whole distance barefooted; but this has fallen into neglect in many cases in the present day, and the easier and more comfortable method of traveling by rail is adopted. Occasionally, however, a pilgrim may be seen measuring the distance with his length.

The doctrine of Transmigration underlies the whole system of Hindu belief—that is, the passage of a human soul through the bodies of many animals. The souls of all animals are held to be those of men, thus degraded on account of their former sins, but capable, after a long succession of births and deaths through long ages, of getting freed from these sins, and attaining final happiness. There is a curious custom prevalent among devout Hindus of feeding the ants, whenever they are found clustering on the surface of the ground, with flour and sugar. It is commonly stated that this is done out of charity, and with a view to preserve life, but we believe it has a deeper meaning, and that the poor deluded man imagines that by so doing he is feeding his mother, or wife, or child, now turned into an ant.

The Hindus are extremely superstitious, and believe in omens, both good and bad. It is considered a good omen, for example, if, on setting out on any business, a man sees a crow fly from left to right, or if he meets two Brahmins, a married woman, or a jackal. It is considered unfavorable, however, if the crow flies from right to left, or if he meets a single Brahmin, a widow, or a cat. A person sneezing, and the sudden extinguishing of a light, are also considered bad omens, but the notes of the lizard are considered a good omen.

Buddhism as such is virtually extinct in South India. Those who call themselves Buddhists are in reality Jains, and are in some respects an offshoot of Buddhism. The Jains deny the divine origin and infallibility of the Vedas, or sacred writings. They believe in a Supreme Being, and revere certain holy men, twenty-four in number, who have acquired, by self-mortification, a station superior to the gods. They show extreme veneration for the sanctity of human life, which they manifest in various ways; they never eat or drink in the dark, for fear they might unconsciously swallow an insect, and thus cause pain to some departed human soul. Some Jains carry a broom, to sweep the ground before they tread on it. Large portions of Hindu mythology are incorporated into the sacred books of the Jains, and the worship at their temples does not differ materially from that at Hindu temples. The Jains are, however, unwilling to be confounded with Hindus who acknowledge caste and Brahminical authority; they never associate with them at festivals nor intermarry; they devote themselves chiefly to commerce and agriculture, and are found in various provinces. The chief priest resides at Chittanur, near Tindivanum, where there is a large Jain temple.

The question is often asked, "What are the feelings which pervade the minds of the Hindus when they worship their deities?" Unquestionably, we think, the predominant feeling is one of fear and apprehension. They fear some calamity will happen to them if they neglect their worship. Educated

Hindus say that they do not in reality worship these dieties, but only the Supreme Being through them. The idea is, however, more speculative than real. At the same time, we cannot help believing that their religion has a monotheistic basis, that is, a belief in the one God, beneath all the "wood, hay, and stubble" of legend and material worship—that they have a vague, indefinable sense of some one Supreme Being who is not far from every one of them. Sometime they had the truth, but, not loving the truth, they substituted the creature for the Creator.

CHAPTER VIII.

HINDU WOMAN.

Her Ideal and Real Status—The Hindu Widow—Female Education and Zenana Work—Female Medical Profession.

THE first piece of knowledge that we have about the women of any branch of the Aryan race is that it was the duty of the maidens of India to milk the cows—a fact revealed by philology when the Sanscrit word "*duhitri*" (daughter) revealed an origin akin to milkmaid. It was considered an honorable office, since the cow, the most invaluable animal to pastoral communities, came to be endowed with almost supernatural attributes. In Vedic times to respect a woman was not only thought to be right, but was also enjoined as a sacred duty. Hard outdoor work was not to be assigned to her, for her place was at the domestic hearth, making it happy by her presence, soothing man in his labors, and consoling him in his sorrow. Man was commanded to protect her with tenderness and please her with gifts. The young girl was free to select the bridegroom of her choice, and her family was bound to provide her with a suitable dowry, to which her brother was recommended to add the finest heifer of his herd, the purest saffron of his crop, and the loveliest jewel in his casket. Her husband should treat her with deference. Husband and wife should go hand in hand into the temple, where the woman offers up fragrant incense upon the altar. Her prayers and hymns were acceptable in the sight of Deity. There was nothing like complete seclusion. Such a thing was neither sanctioned by the Vedas nor did it obtain in practice. In the Vedic age women appeared in public. Some of the most beautiful hymns were written by queens and princesses.

The next landmark in the degradation of women is the Code of Manu, that is to say, the formal promulgation of the Brahminic faith. To the natural preference for male posterity, which is common to all early states of society, there had now succeeded a religious horror at not leaving behind a son, who alone could perform certain ceremonies which were considered essential to secure the parents' final happiness. In "Manu's Institutes" we read that women should be sheltered by the fostering care of their fathers, husbands, and brothers; that eternal misery is in store for those who rob them of their possessions; that every happiness attends the house in which they are happy; that the right-minded man should have but one wife, as the virtuous wife should have but one husband. Manu even declares that "one mother is more venerable

SNAKE CHARMERS.

(*From a native drawing.*)

See pages 59, 60.

than a thousand fathers." The kind and chivalrous treatment of women is inculcated. Manu, while enjoining her to honor her husband and preserve her purity, enjoins also the husband "to have no strife with her," and to consider her as his own body.

Another *rishi* (sage) says, "Strike not even with a blossom a wife guilty of a hundred faults." Moreover, of the eight forms of the nuptial ceremony enumerated by Manu, one form invested females with the power of choosing their future lords. The maids appeared before a large group of men assembled for the purpose, and made their choice, not only by the outward appearance of the men, but by their character, antecedents, and accomplishments.

After Manu came Buddha, who raised the cry against the tyranny of caste and the priestcraft of Brahminism. Men and women were equal, according to his doctrine; but it was not in the pure happiness of home that they should seek salvation. Rather, they should bury themselves in the seclusion of monastic life, and, by destroying passion, and contemplating the Deity, make ready to enter Nirvana, the absorption of the soul into the universal spirit. The mind of Buddha was entirely possessed by the fascination of existence in convents and secluded places; and this was one reason why Buddhism early lost nearly all its quickly-conquered empire in India. It is worthy of remark that in Burmah, where Buddhism has survived, and has preserved something of its original character, women enjoy a large measure of social freedom. Most of the shops, it is said, are kept by women; they are not restricted from conversation with men; the daughters receive the guests, and are allowed every opportunity of seeing their suitors, and are at liberty to marry anyone they like best, whether he be rich or poor.

Next to the purely Vedic writings, the Sanscrit epic poetry is held in the highest honor by the Hindus. The greatest of these poems, the Ramayana, is one long chant in honor of woman's virtue. The other Indian epic, the Mahabaratam, contains a whole gallery of female portraits. We will only quote the words of one personage in the Mahabaratam: "The wife is the honor of the family. The wife is the man's vital spirit, is the man's half, is his best friend, and the source of all his felicity. The wife with her endearing discourse is the friend in solitude, the mother to the oppressed, and a refreshment on the journey in the wilderness of life."

The first signs of woman's degradation in India date back to a time anterior to the Christian era; its consummation was the work of those repeated Moslem invasions which took place during the tenth and succeeding centuries. The march of Mohammedanism has been the bane of women. The social position of women in India at the present time is to a great extent one of degradation; they are regarded very much in the light of goods and chattels. They are largely distrusted, and are kept in check by a jealous, perpetual oversight. A husband never seems willing to trust his wife out of his sight. Should they walk out together, they do not proceed side by side, on an equality with each other, but the wife either goes a few steps in advance of her lord, who follows as her jealous guardian and protector, or else follows her husband a few steps behind, like a slave. She is usually addressed with abrupt harshness, and obeys with obsequious docility. If there is any burden to be carried, she is made to carry it, while he walks free and unburdened.

The rules of social life in regard to the sexes are so strict that it is contrary to a Hindu's notions of etiquette and propriety to inquire after the health of his wife and daughters. English people often seriously offend in this respect on their first arrival in the country. With regard to the female sex, strict silence is imposed. Should a male friend call on his neighbor, the wife retires until he departs. Women, generally speaking, do not associate with men, and are rarely spoken to by them. There is no such thing as courtship in India. A Hindu rarely sees his wife, and certainly never talks to her before their marriage. It is manifest, therefore, that jealousy and fear have a much stronger influence over the minds of a Hindu husband and wife than love and friendship. Love may and often does spring up afterwards, but at the commencement of married life there cannot be any bond of affection between them.

The birth of a female is not hailed with joy, but deplored as a calamity. She is treated as an inferior, subjected to privations, exposed to insults, lost in the slough of superstition, fleeced by priests, and victimized by relatives. Childhood is the only period of real joy which a Hindu girl has. She is then free to play about as she pleases, never troubled to learn anything but what she can pick up from the women about her, and both petted and spoiled by her relatives. But this season of happiness soon comes to an end. At the age of twelve or thirteen the spoiled child is sent off against her will to join her husband's family, entering it, not as American brides enter their future homes, at the head of the female community, but at the bottom. Child though she still is, her childhood is past forever, and she is transformed into a young woman, too often by no means a happy one. Seclusion adds to the sorrows of her existence.

Hindu women from the time they give up their childhood to the time of their death are to a large extent kept apart from the public, and live an aimless life. They lounge about from place to place. They spend their time, after household duties have been attended to, mostly in putting up their hair and pulling it down again, in putting on their jewels and taking them off again. The only excitement they have is a quarrel, which comes once in a while to relieve the monotony of their existence. But while saying all this, we do not admit that they have no influence. Theoretically they may be of no account, but practically they are often all in all. In many cases the supreme rulers are mothers-in-law, who rule their subjects with a rod of iron, or else an ignorant, superstitious grandmother is the secret wire puller, who arranges everything according to her own sweet will.

But hard as the lot of an ordinary Hindu woman is, that of a Hindu widow is tenfold worse. It is said that there are twenty-one million widows in India, and half of them are virgin widows. They are deprived of all that women value in this world, their ornaments are taken away, they are dressed in very coarse clothing, their hair shorn off, they are made to subsist on the coarsest food, compelled to fast till health breaks down, kept from joining in any amusements, forced to be the unpaid drudge of the family, considered fit only to amuse the children, and taught to consider themselves as creatures of ill omen. How much Hindu women dread widowhood is shown in the fact that to call a woman a widow is to offer her a dire insult. It is the custom of infant betrothal and child marriage which entails the greatest misery upon the women of India, and is at the root of every other. It is the obstacle to the spread of education, the stumbling-block in the way of Christianity, and the cause of hundreds of thousands of child widows. Stunted growth, disease, lack of stamina, of moral energy and physical ability, are a few of the evils attributable to this source.

But a great change has come over the better spirits of the country within recent years. There was a time—not many years ago—when a woman's personal attractions and culinary achievements were regarded as constituting her sole claim to attention, and her mind was thought incapable of culture. It was thought improper to send a girl to a public school—nay, a source of positive harm. For a woman to learn poetry, music, and art, and to be known to possess a knowledge of these things, was to stamp her in the eyes of all men as low and vile. A virtuous woman in India was an ignorant domestic drudge. The education of women was wholly foreign to the tradition and usages of the people, and they looked with suspicion on the new-fangled but well-meant efforts of the English to raise their womankind out of the slough of ignorance, to which their sages had agreed to consign them, as the safest and most virtuous place for the sex to occupy.

Looking at all the facts of the case, and considering what the habits of thought of the people really are, it is not a little remarkable that so much has been already effected in the way of female education. A few years ago schools were opened, at which the attendance of a few girls of the poorest families was obtained by a system of rewards which was very much like paying them for attending school. Gradually these female schools began to take deeper root, and to exert an influence on more influential portions of the community.

After some years the plan of giving rewards for attendance was given up, the education only being given. Some time afterwards the parents were induced to supply the materials for education, such as slates, books, etc. Still later a small fee, and then a larger, and yet a larger one, was charged, until now the amount thus raised, though far too small, is sufficient to afford considerable help in bearing the whole burden of these school expenses. And, better than this, the idea of female education has taken such a hold that the Hindus are themselves engaging in it. But female education is entirely a growth of the new time, and can be expected to flourish only among the new generation of the educated and enlightened. Progress will be made in the centers of activity and knowledge first, and afterwards in the more retired towns and villages.

For some time it was a serious question how to reach the women of the better classes, who were secluded in certain apartments, or large houses called zenanas, and were not allowed to appear in public like women of inferior rank. The difficulty was solved by the wives of missionaries visiting these native ladies, and there imparting instruction to them. In this way access has been gained to thousands of families of good social position, and large numbers of females connected with them are receiving a useful secular and Christian education.

Several societies have been established for the express object of sending out well-educated Christian young ladies, from Britain and America, to labor in this important department. Educated Hindu young men, also, seeing the position occupied by English ladies in their families by virtue of their education, have become anxious that their own wives should be as well educated, and thus become companions to them, and not mere ciphers and drudges.

Nevertheless, it should not be forgotten that, as regards the great mass of the female population, very little has yet been done for their education and enlightenment. According to the report of the director of public instruction of Madras for 1885–86, the number of females at school was fifty-eight thousand seven hundred and ninety-seven. Large and encouraging as this may seem, it represents only about three in a hundred of the girls of school-going age. From the returns for 1887–88, just issued, it appears that there were sixty-four thousand three hundred and twenty-eight girls in public schools, and eight hundred in private schools.

These numbers, it is true, represent only the pupils in schools wnich furnish returns to the government; but even supposing that there are as many more under instruction in other schools, a very small proportion of the girls has been reached.

Besides, the great majority of the pupils are in the primary department, showing that parents do not yet permit their daughters to share as fully in the advantages of education as they ought to do. Further, there is a great lack of well-qualified female teachers, and of pure, healthy, instructive literature for females to read. But the progress of female education and the beneficent zenana mission work cannot now be arrested. Present advance is great, and future prospects are bright.

We must not forget to mention the beneficent scheme inaugurated by Lady Dufferin, which has for its object the provision of medical aid for females. The women of India have become accustomed to the idea that it is now possible to obtain the services of a trained medical attendant of their own sex, and the calling of a lady doctor has taken its place among the liberal professions of the country. The scheme has succeeded beyond the most sanguine expectations of its promoters. Already there are more than two hundred and twenty female students in the Indian medical schools, and the demand for aid is greater than can be met. No one acquainted with the untold sufferings and miseries of Hindu women, arising from malpractices and the reckless waste of human life resulting therefrom, can doubt that it is destined to be fraught with great good to the country.

Madras has always taken a foremost place in the provision of medical education for women, and was the first to open the doors of its local medical college to them. Already from it four candidates have graduated in medicine, several have qualified for lower grades, and some have proceeded to Britain to complete their studies.

Girls are being educated, some are being trained as medical women, and Christian households are being formed. As Professor Monier Williams says: "Hope for India lies in this. The missionary band must carry the ark persistently round the Indian home, until its walls are made to fall, and its inner life exposed to the fresh air of God's day, and all its surroundings moulded after the pattern of a pure, healthy, Christian household, whose influences leaven the life of a family and the nation from the cradle to the grave." Who can estimate what change for the better will be wrought when a new generation shall have arisen, and those who are now the pupils of schools will have become the heads of many households, the mothers of future generations? Christian charity cannot sow in more promising fields than the institutions which mould the minds and hearts of the females of India. A terse Tamil proverb says, "As is the thread, so is the cloth; as is the mother, so is the child;" and a bright future is in store for India, now that the future mothers of the country are beginning, in so large a proportion, to pass under the influence of education. The women of India represent the solid strength of Hinduism. The soul of superstition has its home in the bosoms of Hindu mothers. It must be assailed there in its native strength if we would conquer India for Christ.

It is from the mother that the child receives its first impulse along the paths of virtue, and it is by educating the mother that a great and powerful nation is most surely created.

We believe that India is on the eve of great changes, or, rather, of rapid progress in this department, and that the church of Christ ought, by means of female schools, and a mission to the zenanas, to take an active and earnest share in aiding it. There is no movement of greater interest, or more hopeful in its results, than that of female education, whether in schools or in zenanas. Better days are at hand; it is the morning that cometh, and not the night; the summer, and not the winter, that draweth nigh; and in the future, when the downtrodden females of India will arise, as by a social regeneration, and stand erect in their recovered womanhood, it will be seen that while the deliverance has come in many ways, yet the Christian and philanthropic societies of Britain and America have played no unimportant part in hastening on that happy time.

CHAPTER IX.

SOME TRAITS OF HINDU CHARACTER.

Virtues of the Hindus—Their Vices and Evils: (1) Untruthfulness and Deceit; (2) Debt; (3) Insincerity and Love of Money; (4) Credulity and Superstition; (5) Love of Display and Fame.

ONE cannot fail to notice the many excellent traits in the Hindu character. Many of them are lovable in many ways. While they are subtle and acute, there is also much that is good and true, such as their patient perseverance, calm endurance under suffering, filial obedience, reverence for superiors, tenderness towards animal life, faithfulness in service, and toleration of religious differences. They have great power of self-restraint and consider it to be a mark of a true religious nature to be free from anger under provocation. They not infrequently argue with the sole purpose of ruffling one's temper. If they succeed in so doing, you have fallen greatly in their estimation; if not, they consider you to be a virtuous man. On one occasion we were arguing with some Brahmins, who were doing their utmost to excite our temper; we managed, however, to preserve our equanimity.

Afterwards a man in the crowd said to his friend, "He does not get angry." "No," said the other; "they do not send out people who get angry!" The higher and middle classes are cleanly both in their persons and in their attire. They are civil and polite in their manners, though it must be admitted that this is often put on, and does not necessarily imply any real regard or affection.

Bishop Caldwell, an experienced missionary, speaking of native Christians in India, says: "I maintain they have no need to shrink from comparison with Christians in a similar station in life, and similarly circumstanced, in England, or in any other part of the world. I think I do not exaggerate when I say that they appear to me in general more teachable, more considerate of the feelings of others, and more respectful to superiors, more temperate, more patient and gentle, more trustful in Providence, better church-goers, yet free from religious bigotry, and, in proportion to their means, more liberal than Christians in England holding a similar position in the social scale. I do not for a moment pretend that they are free from imperfections; but when I have compared them with what I have seen and known of Christians in other countries, I find that their good qualities have left a deeper impression on my mind than their imperfections."

It is of the utmost importance both on social and political grounds that a good feeling should exist between the European rulers and the natives of the country. Not infrequently young civil and military servants, on their first arrival in India, despise and ill treat the Hindus, as though they were a savage and ignorant people rather than an enlightened and civilized one. Would it not be wise for all who expect to go to India to remember that they are going, not to a barbarous and savage country, but to a country famous for its antiquity and civilization, and having among its inhabitants good and intelligent men who deserve to be treated with kindness and consideration?

But admiration for the many excellent qualities of the Hindus should not blind us to their defects and failings. The leading national vices and evils of the country appear to us to be the following:—

1. *Lying and Deceit.*—While not going so far as Lord Macaulay in thinking that "deceit is to a Hindu what beauty is to a woman, what a sting is to a bee, and what a horn is to a buffalo," yet one cannot fail to be struck with this all-pervading evil. It is hydra-headed, and pervades the country through and through. It meets you everywhere and in various forms. Your own house servants, outwardly respectful and obsequious, deceive you every day of their lives. A man comes to see you, and you question him on some matter; he will hardly ever give you a straightforward answer, but will try to discover what reply you wish, and will answer accordingly, without the slightest regard as to whether it is true or not. Honesty and truth

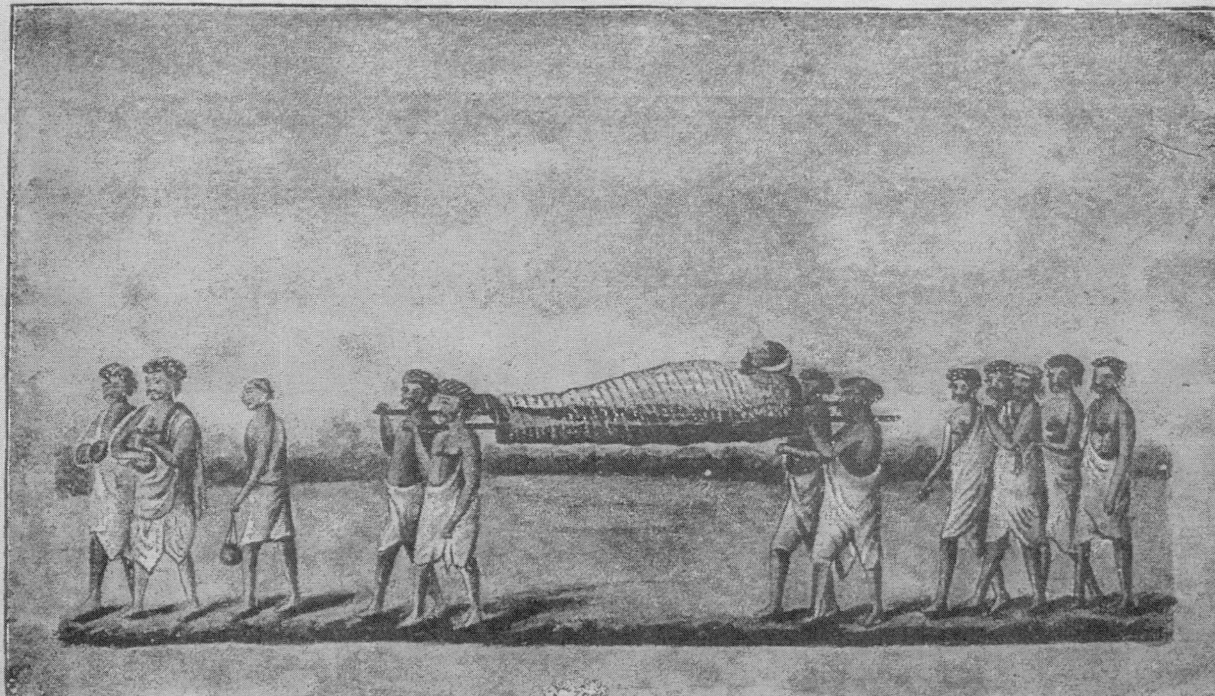

A FUNERAL.

(From a native drawing.)

See page 69.

are little understood and appreciated. A Hindu has little more idea of truth than a blind man of color. His moral sense has become so dull that he mistakes for truth that which goes by that name among the people with whom he lives.

2. *Debt.*—This is another evil widely prevalent. Almost all classes are involved in debt—those with fixed salaries as well as those whose incomes are fluctuating and precarious. This is the normal condition of the people. The native of India is almost always in debt; if he is not, it is generally because no one will lend him anything. There is a proverb in Tamil, that "where there is no debt there is no honor." We once heard of a village near Delhi where the people were poor and free from debt. A canal was made; the value of the land increased; the people became prosperous, and also became involved in debt. The reason why they were not in debt before was that the land was too poor to afford security, but as soon as the value of the land improved, they at once got into debt.

Marriage and funeral expenses are the chief causes of debt. A man drawing a salary of ten rupees a month will not hesitate to borrow one hundred rupees or two hunded rupees at twelve per cent interest to celebrate his marriage, the whole of which is spent in presents and festivities. Farmers borrow money to pay their rents to the government. The money lender is always ready to lend, provided the man is in service, and able to pay the interest monthly from his wages. This evil pervades the Christian church also, and it will take some time before it is eradicated.

3. *Insincerity, Selfishness, and Love of Money.*—Most Hindus live a double life. Abroad they are freethinkers—reformers—at home they are far different. They expound excellent principles of morality, and have just views of men and things, but in the midst of their domestic surroundings do the very things they so zealously denounced elsewhere. Personally they may disbelieve in astrology, but when any important work is to be performed they do it on some auspicious day determined beforehand by an astrologer.

Many of them believe in their inmost souls that the ceremonies performed by the family priest, and the prayers uttered by him, are a sham, and a mockery, yet they submit to them, for fear of being reviled as apostates from the ancestral faith.

They know that the best thing they can do for their sons is to keep them single until they can earn for themselves enough to maintain wife and children; but such is the tyranny of custom that they must get them married as soon as they arrive at man's estate, even though they themselves have to bear the burden of supporting them and all the children they may bring into existence.

As to their selfishness and love of money, Rajah Sir Madava Roa gives the following picture: "The accumulation of money becomes a life passion. In the eager pursuit of wealth the conditions of health are neglected. No exercise is taken. No recreation is resorted to. The man takes no leave. He denies himself change of place, climate, and scene. He is irregular as regards food, sleep, and other necessary functions. He denies himself all personal enjoyment by a rigorous parsimony. If friends call upon him, he says he is very busy, and sends them away. He grows increasingly fat as time goes on. Health being neglected, he is blessed with few or no children. He denies assistance to poor and suffering relatives. His ideal is to accumulate a certain large sum of money. He is reluctant to retire from business or work, and clings to the same with fatal tenacity. Diseases and infirmities creep in, but are unnoticed. Doctors and friends give gentle hints, but in vain. In the absorbing passion for money, he has not contemplated the uncertainty of life. He is suddenly overtaken with sickness, and is quite unable to make his will. Shortly after he dies, unregretted, and is soon forgotten. Denying all enjoyment to himself, he has denied it to friends, family, and relatives. The long-accumulated money goes to idlers or vicious persons. A flood of litigation ensues, and money is dissipated in a hundred ways." A sad picture, but true.

4. *Credulity and Superstition.*—This is another prominent trait in the Hindu character. They not only believe the most absurd stories contained in their religious books, but any marvelous story they

hear is at once credited, without ever questioning its truth. They believe that there are holy men (*rishis*) living in certain places who perform most wonderful miracles, though they have never witnessed any one of them.

They are superstitious to a large degree—superstition binds them hand and foot. Whenever they take any important step in life, such as weddings, journeys, education of children, a priest is always consulted as to whether the time is auspicious or not. They are hedged in by fears and prejudices on all sides. Dreading their priest, their deities, and daily portents, their lives are rendered bitter by a ceaseless anxiety to avoid some malicious fortune, they know not what.

5. *Love of Display and of Fame.*—This passion is peculiar to all classes, and large sums of money are spent in its gratification. They build temples, rest houses for travelers (*chattrams*), dig wells, plant groves of mangoes, and such like, all for the sake of fame and with a love of display. They give away alms to the poor, and feed many Brahmins, in order to get praise of men. They always let their right hand know what their left hand does. They would rather give away a large sum publicly than a small sum privately.

Their love of display manifests itself in their dress, their marriage ceremonies, and their daily official life. Every petty official has one or two attendants waiting on him, whilst the simplicity of attire of the highest European officials, and the quiet, unostentatious way in which they frequently move about the country, fills them with astonishment. To see a European walking instead of riding seems strange and incongruous to them.

We have often been accosted, when walking out in the country, with the remark, "You are walking!" as much as to imply you ought to be riding. Frequently when we have gone into a village to preach, and have left our vehicle or horse by the roadside, the remark has been addressed to us in surprise and wonderment, "Have you come walking?"

CHAPTER X.

EDUCATION.

Education and Preaching Mutually Supplementary, not Antagonistic—Notwithstanding Rapid Progress of Education Ignorance Still a National Evil—Great Need cf Technical Schools—Importance of Education as an Evangelistic Agency—Its Fruits—Attitude of Educated Young Men towards Christianity—Desire of the Natives Themselves for a *Complete* Education, Religious and Secular—Need for Some Special Evangelistic Agency in Every Missionary Institution—A Larger Use of the Press Desirable.

INDIA is a unique country. It is vast in extent, and teeming with population. It is the home at once of the highest mental faculties and the grossest superstition. It is the stronghold of social principles which spread through every grade of the community, penetrate every crevice of the popular life, and deprave and paralyze the people, restraining all free thought and action. It is a country in which all forms of labor require to be persistently and patiently carried on. Its compact masses must be widely and deeply moved by the gospel before converts are made in large numbers. Preaching and teaching are the two main forms of Christian effort. They are sometimes set one against the other, as though they were mutually antagonistic. We have engaged in both, believe in both, and both have been attended with beneficial results. We regard them as mutually helpful. To the influence, on the one hand, of education in moulding the opinions of the people may be attributed the feeling of greater kindness with which the preachers of the gospel are received. On the other hand, not a few who may have received their first impressions in a mission school have had those impressions deepened and quickened by attending the meetings and hearing the lectures and addresses of the distinctively preaching missionary.

Fifty years have passed away since Lord Macaulay's "Minute" settled in favor of the English language the controversy which had long been raging as to whether the highest form of education given by the government to the people of India ought to be in the oriental classical languages of the country or in English. Though that Minute was the source whence the great movement in favor of English education originated, yet little was done beyond the establishment of a high school in each presidency, and the starting of a few mission schools, till the famous dispatch of Sir Charles Wood (late Lord Halifax), which may be regarded as the Magna Charta of Indian education. That dispatch laid down the principle that as the work of education was too great to be accomplished by the government alone, committees of native gentlemen and missionary and philanthropic societies should be encouraged, by a system of grants in aid of their schools, to co-operate in the great work. It also enacted that universities, after the model of the London University, should be established in the three presidency cities of Calcutta, Madras, and Bombay. This was done in 1857, and since then the development of education has been great. Village schools, high schools, and colleges, of a class similar to those existing in England, are flourishing in every direction over large tracts of country. The people are being gradually educated in the highest forms of knowledge according to the best-known methods of Europe. An educated class, with ideas of progress, virtue, and freedom, drawn from the fountains of English literature, has sprung up, and the mental slavery of former times has received its death blow.

Education in conjunction with Christianity is revolutionizing India. Notwithstanding this progress, however, ignorance is still a national evil. According to the educational report of the Madras presidency for 1885–86, the total number of schools and colleges furnishing returns to the department was sixteen thousand and fourteen, containing three hundred and ninety-seven thousand and forty male and fifty-eight thousand seven hundred and ninety-seven female scholars. These numbers are no doubt

A WOMAN DECORATING HER DOORSTEP.

(From a native drawing.)

See page 89.

in themselves large, but yet they represent only one-sixth of the boys and one-thirty-fifth of the girls of a school-going age. The total number of children reading in primary schools on March 31, 1886, was four hundred and nineteen thousand one hundred and seventy-three, which was less than one-eleventh of those between six and eleven years of age. From the returns for 1887–88, issued by the government of Madras, which we have just seen, it appears that there were four hundred and sixty-four thousand six hundred and fifty-four boys under instruction in public institutions, of whom only one-sixteenth were pupils of colleges, whereas almost ninety-two in every hundred were receiving instruction in primary schools and classes.

As has been well said: "The leaven of education has only just begun to work, and the lump to be leavened is a bewildering mass. It works, too, under conditions of extreme difficulty, connected with the social customs and general poverty of the people. It is too early to expect a general renaissance of intellectual life in India. The work to be done has been, and still is, to a large extent, destructive. The ground has to be cleared of weeds and the ruins of centuries of ignorance and apathy, before the foundation of a genuine national intellectual life can be laid. But the forces are at work which tend surely, if slow'y, to that end. The overturning process is going on with ever-increasing energy. The influence of Western religious thought on its ethical sides as an organ of intellectual and political movement, is steadily introducing higher ideals of life, a more adequate conception of duty, and a sense of the dignity of responsibility. The movement is slow, but it is one which gathers impetus as it proceeds. Meanwhile there is a good deal which may be done in the improvement of the highest class of teaching power."

The great need of the country at the present time is the establishment of technical schools for the instruction of the people in various mechanical industries. The present system of education is too wholly literary. Far better make the son of a farmer a better farmer, and the son of an artisan a better artisan, than, by withdrawing them from the plow and the workshop, create a class of discontented place seekers clamoring for government employment, while all such avenues to public employment are more than crowded.

As has been already stated, this form of missionary work is often looked upon with suspicion, because imperfectly understood. In our opinion, a mission without provision for high-class missionary education would be as vitally defective as a mission with no provision for preaching the gospel in the vernacular or native tongue. There you have a class of hearers in the most impressible period of life. There are no disturbers to interrupt. The congregation is always the same—the same minds are daily acted upon. The doctrines of Christianity are presented in their connection and mutual bearings. Truth is taught, not in fragments but in a system. Above all, Christian character and Christian example, in their living, visible power, are brought to bear on the truth. The congregation not only hears but sees Christianity. Moreover, you have there a class of Hindu society possessing wealth and influence, which no other mission agency at present at work would adequately influence.

But the success of education as a missionary agency depends entirely on the efficiency of the religious instruction given, and on the *personal* influence which the missionary brings to bear on the scholars. Where this is properly done, the work is successful. Further, the number of Christian masters should always be sufficient to give the school a Christian tone and character. The present writer's experience embraces both preaching in the native tongue and English education, and, while expressing a preference for the former, he has resolutely set himself against the idea that a missionary teacher is not doing missionary work as truly and thoroughly as any of his brethren. By means of the educational institutions of the country, Hinduism is being "killed through its brain," as Dr. Duff used to say. The growth of mind and enlarged knowledge thus attained exert a direct influence on their position as Hindus. They tend to weaken and destroy national and family prejudices, to expose the selfishness and tyranny of caste, to put down the pretensions of the Brahminical priesthood, and to thoroughly undermine the popular idolatry. The young men trained in mission schools manifest in many ways the fruit of their Christian education. Though not converted men, many live a superior moral life, and are distinguished above those around them for truthfulness, gentleness, uprightness, diligence in business, and a desire to benefit others. They are convinced that if any religion on earth be true, it is Christianity. Yet they remain in name Hindus, quietly observing so much of the current idolatries, ceremonies, and customs of their families as the public opinion around compels them to follow, and waiting for the good time when the universal change will set them free.

A missionary states that a short time ago he came in contact with a young Hindu gentleman who was a graduate of the university. He was a Brahmin of the highest caste, and his father had been likewise a Brahmin of the highest caste, and highly educated. This young man said that when his father was dying, he called his children round his bed, and said to them, "If you should ever change your religion, you must become Christians, because," he said, "I do not know whether any religion is true, but if any it is Christianity." That is a remarkable confession from the apparently unbroken citadel of Brahminism. Besides, the teaching of government and secular colleges destroys the ancestral faith without supplying a better. It turns multitudes of educated young men into disciples of Bradlaugh and Ingersoll, whose writings are widely circulated among them. Missionaries are driven, therefore, in self-defense to maintain a firm and aggressive attitude against the cultured infidelity which is honeycombing the upper and middle classes of Hindu society. If we wish to preserve India from falling from "gods many and lords many" into a state of utter godlessness, it is essential to maintain some well-manned missionary institutions—manned not by *mere scholars*, but by *earnest Christians*.

We believe that no greater disaster could happen to India at the present time than the withdrawal of missionaries altogether from the higher education of the country. We trust that none of the great societies will be induced to do so by the appeals, however importunate, of these arm-chair critics.

Moreover, it is a remarkable circumstance that the Hindus will in many cases more readily send their sons to mission schools, where they know they will receive a Christian as well as a secular education, than to the government schools, where they will receive only secular instruction. Popular as the system of government education is, there is this general objection to it on the part of the natives, that it undermines and overthrows their long-cherished religious convictions—it has removed the swaddling bands of Indian morality, such as they are—without supplying others in their place. They consider it strange, if not improper, on the part of government to exclude religion from the course of study pursued in its institutions. The Maharajah of Mysore, in a speech made at the distribution of prizes at the Mysore College, said: "I must confess to a feeling of anxiety in my mind that the education given in our schools and colleges is one-sided, and that unless supplemented by an education calculated to arouse and develop the emotional and religious element in our nature, it cannot raise the moral or even the intellectual tone of our society, or purify the national taste, or refine the intercourse of private life." It cannot be denied that there can be no complete education unless religious and secular instruction are combined.

It should be mentioned that there is a tendency, which ought to be carefully guarded against, of religious instruction in mission schools being encroached upon, owing to the increasing demands of university education. As has been well said: "Schools thoroughly aflame with evangelistic life are of great missionary value. But the tendency of the mere intellectual to crowd out the spiritual, the head to starve and enfeeble the heart, demands watchfulness and extreme care." Every missionary institution should, therefore, have some special gospel agency working side by side with it, for the purpose of following up and deepening impressions on those who have been at one time under instruction, but who, being engaged in the battle of life, have no one to remind them of the lessons then learned, or to quicken the impressions then made. The educational work is manifestly one-sided and inadequate so long as there is no such agency working in conjunction with it, for the express purpose of meeting with those in whose heart the seed of divine truth has been already sown, and who may be unconsciously longing for something more satisfying than the world can give. If every mission were to set apart an able foreign missionary and a well-educated, English-speaking native evangelist to devote their whole time to visiting this class of natives in their homes, receiving visits in return, holding meetings and Bible-classes among students and among non-Christian teachers, delivering public lectures and addresses, and having social gatherings, much good would accrue, and some choice sheaves for the great Master would be brought out.

A freer, fuller use should also be made of the press. The stream of atheistic and corrupting literature rushes with unabated force through the government offices and colleges, bearing before it much of the heart and genius of the rising generation of the country. Skeptical, or, rather, professedly antichristian, books of the lowest and least reputable kind, which offer no truth in the place of that they attempt to destroy, find a ready market among men educated or half educated in the English language. In the present condition of India, when thought is awakening on so many subjects, when public opinion is forming, and when so much literature of unhealthy character is being widely scattered, it is the duty of the Christian church to guide as far as possible the current of opinion, and to diffuse by means of the press a Christian spirit and a knowledge of Christian truth.

CHAPTER XI.

EVANGELISTIC WORK.

Paramount Importance of Preaching—The Best Times and Methods to be Adopted in Preaching—Some Arguments and Discussions—Concentration of Effort Desirable—Christian Literature Should Be Widely Circulated—Results of Bazaar Preaching.

THE preaching of the gospel to the Hindus in their own tongue is rightly regarded as the principal duty of a missionary's life, and is obviously the most natural way of spreading the gospel. The most suitable times for preaching in India are the early morning and at sunset. The streets are then crowded with people, arrayed in many colors, but chiefly white, all walking about and talking. The noise of an Indian street is like the "noise of many waters," but it mostly proceeds from human voices. Shops line both sides of the street, where merchants, in a large or small way of business, sitting generally under the shade of a thatch or bamboo screen, shout the excellence of their wares. People pass and repass in an endless stream. Here a small group of artisans; there a little knot of clerks in white flowing garments making their way to or from the public offices; here coolies carrying burdens, and there belted government officials bearing messages, with many others of various occupations and employments.

Into the midst of this gay and confused throng the Christian preacher with his assistant makes his way, and takes his stand under the shade of some tree or on some vacant spot by the side of the public road. It is usual to commence with the reading of a passage of Scripture or the singing of some Christian song with or without instrumental accompaniment. The people are passionately fond of music, and a crowd immediately gathers. We do not take a text, and say "firstly, secondly, then thirdly, and finally one word in conclusion," but we talk to the people in a simple, homely, conversational way. How much better, also, the adoption of this course would be in many congregations in Christian lands!

The addresses in all effective bazaar preaching are short—not more than fifteen minutes or so each. The best and usual plan is to have three or four short addresses, interspersed with singing. The preacher needs to be wise as a serpent, and to strike forcibly. The most telling addresses are those which make free use of quotations from their sacred books and are full of pointed illustrations. Imagination is to a Hindu very much like his second self, and analogies glitter on the thread of his talk like the beads of a necklace. They know little or nothing of logic, and long, elaborate processes of reasoning are a mere waste of time. Many an audience has been dispersed by dry and prolonged expositions of the ten commandments and such like.

It is not safe, moreover, to conclude that because an audience listens patiently it is, therefore, interested. It has happened on more than one occasion that an audience has listened for some time, apparently with rapt attention, to a missionary addressing them *in their own language*, and at the end have quietly informed the speaker that they are unacquainted with English! It is possible for a Hindu to have his whole soul apparently absorbed in a subject, and yet for his real thoughts to be as far from it as the east is from the west.

The speaker is not allowed to speak for long, as a general rule, without someone interrupting him to ask a question or raise an objection. The Hindu is naturally fond of argumentation on religious topics, and the crowd always becomes denser as soon as a discussion is started. All such discussions should be firmly declined until the close. The questions are frequently very shrewd and are generally asked for the sake of testing the ability of the speaker, and have no serious purpose about them. Those who ask them are usually not in earnest; the questions are merely surface inquiries with them, and not blood questions. As a specimen of some of their arguments the following may be given :—

"You say that the Christian religion is the only true religion. Now we see as a matter of fact that

A FEMALE WATER CARRIER.

(From a native drawing.)

there are many religions in the world, just as there are many different kinds of fruit. There is the mango, guava, custard apple, and the plantain. Each has a peculiar taste and sweetness of its own. Some prefer one, some another. So it is with the different religions of the world. Some prefer one, and some another, according to their taste and idiosyncrasy. Your religion is good for you, and ours for us." All arguments, however, are not equally good. Speaking once on the absurdity of idolatry, we illustrated it by pointing out how they took a stone, and, after breaking it into two pieces, placed one on the doorstep and trod upon it, while the other was carved into an image and worshiped. To this the reply was that there was nothing incongruous in such a thing, for here were two women—one was our wife, the other our mother-in-law; the one we respected, the other we kicked!

Our teachings in the mission field are, for the most part, elementary. The being and fatherhood of God, the sin of idolatry, and the sinfulness of all sin, the gift of a Saviour, and the main facts of our Lord's life, his dying for our sins, his resurrection and ascension, his mediation and return to judgment, repentance and faith, the regenerating work of the Holy Spirit, the nature of Christian worship and Christian life—these are the doctrines most frequently insisted on. The people hear these truths proclaimed; some receive the message, purchase our Christian books, become inquirers and afterward converts. But large numbers listen to the preaching, acknowledge its truth, laugh at their idols, and go away unconcerned.

The question is often raised as to the best method of preaching the gospel in India. Our own belief and practice have been to recognize what is good and true in the Eastern religions, and to enforce the necessity of the whole gospel of Jesus Christ for saving lost souls. "The gospel preached to the Hindus should be in adaptation to those relics as much as the integrity of the truth will allow, and not as little as human ignorance or caprice will tolerate." We believe that whatever is true in Hinduism will leap forth in responsive echo to its complement as exhibited in Christ, and will prove its truth by uniting with it. The glory of Christianity consists in this, that it spreads its tent over the whole of mankind, and everything that is true to the instincts of mankind is expressed, enforced, and established in Christianity.

Again, the question is often asked whether, in addressing the Hindus, the errors of their system should be exposed. To this we reply in the words of one well acquainted with India: "Unquestionably, if the Hindus were a serious, reflecting people, deeply in earnest in religious matters, it might be sufficient to set forth simply the excellency of the Christian religion, and leave the people to discover the deficiency of their own systems. But seeing that they are blinded by their own idolatrous creed and prejudices, that their reasoning powers have for long ages been warped by evil principles, that they scarcely understand how, when two principles are mutually contradictory, one must be given up as false, nothing else than a clear statement of the truth and a full exposure of evil will induce them to see and receive the gospel as a message of glad tidings. A surgical operation is necessary before the cataract can be removed from their spiritual vision, and this operation is the exposure of the errors of their system. At the same time this should be done in such a way as not needlessly to excite their ill-will or wound their feelings. 'With the wisdom of the serpent should be united the harmlessness of the dove."

Besides preaching in the streets and bazaars, missionaries make use of lecture halls, rooms, and small buildings erected by the side of the public thoroughfares, called *zayats*, which are lighted with lanterns hung from the roof or upon its supporting posts, and which present an attractive appearance when lighted up in the evening. This gives order, system, and convenience to the efforts of the missionary.

Instead of formal proclamations from platforms and such like, a good plan adopted by some missionaries is what may be called the Socratic method, namely, to get into the very midst of the people and begin by asking them questions. The same questions may be put again and again, till a few truths are fairly deposited in the minds of some, at least. In this way one finds out what they know and what they do not know. Great benefit also results from appealing to one's own experience when preaching to the heathen. Though we may not be able to convince them by logical argument of the truths we proclaim, we can say, I *know* that I have realized this and that; and a positive utterance of that kind always carries with it a certain amount of weight.

As the teaching of the mass of the people the principal facts and doctrines of the Christian faith is the great need of India, tours, or itinerancies, are made into the surrounding towns and villages. Every such vernacular preacher takes a certain limited tract of country and works it regularly and systematically, making a stay of ten days or so in chief towns, leaving no part of the place unvisited. Thus by constant preaching or conversation he gives all a chance of hearing, and at the same time visits all the villages within a radius of several miles. After having worked this tract of country, he passes on to "the regions beyond," adopting a similar plan. Such a method, though slow, brings the missionary into close contact with the people, and secures a deposit of truth often fertile in permanent results. The greatness and worth of such a method repeated over a whole country's breadth cannot be overestimated.

The great fairs and festivals of the county are

also visited. The good seed of the kingdom sown amid the noise and confusion of the bazaar and the crowded festival has sometimes found the "good ground," and yielded fruit to the glory of God; but we believe experience bears out the fact that village visitation faithfully followed up has yielded a larger harvest than evangelistic toil in such places, or even in the larger cities and towns. The greater quiet and decorum which prevail in these little village congregations, gathered together in the veranda of some private dwelling or in the village headman's house, make the preacher feel that his words go straighter to the mark, and are not beaten back into his face, as in the noisy bazaar or the crowded fair.

In all our evangelistic efforts an important help is the selling of Christian books and tracts. The missionary should remain for a time among the people after the preaching is over, engage in familiar conversation with them, visit the principal houses, and either sell a Christian book or leave a tract behind. This has been our invariable custom. It requires great tact and patience, but the missionary should personally engage in it, and thus encourage the native helpers.

The divine blessing on the printed page, without the voice of the living preacher to enforce and explain its teaching, has been so marked in India that every effort should be made to extend the circulation of good books.

The results of preaching are not few. To hundreds and thousands Christianity is no longer a new and "strange doctrine," but a familiar topic of conversation and discussion. Intelligent questions about the leading doctrines of Christianity prove that it has been pondered by thinking minds. Confidence in pagan myths and hoary superstitions has been manifestly shaken, open opposition has signally decreased, and a higher-toned morality is spreading among the people.

In many places leading men, though unprepared to break the shackles of caste and ancient usage, do not hesitate publicly to declare their conviction that the Puranas are false and the Bible is true. A good feeling towards Christianity prevails more and more widely among the people; Christian principles, apart from the facts and doctrines on which they are based, are becoming more and more popular; people speculate as to the possible or probable Christianization of the whole country a century hence; actual converts from all classes have been made; many promise that they will openly profess themselves Christians at some future time, and there are large numbers of secret disciples who have broken with their idols, and given up many heathen customs connected therewith, who have kissed, as it were, the hem of Christ's garment and passed on, but have not moral courage to come out entirely and confess themselves on the Lord's side. We often hear of men who have caught up some stray word, or received a tract from some passing missionary, and who, having carried away the seed in their hearts, have been living almost as Christians remote from all churches and unknown by any. Distance in some cases and timidity in others swell the ranks of those secret disciples. Though their names are not written in the roll-calls of our churches, or in missionary reports and statistics, they are none the less the real disciples of Christ.

When we reflect upon the many false ideas on all subjects exploded, the amount of accurate knowledge imparted, the spirit of thought and inquiry aroused, the love of purity and truth excited, the restraint imposed on open wickedness, the prejudices removed, the accustoming of the people to the very terms of the gospel, and the causing of new ideas of truth to enter into their minds, in however crude a form; when we think, also, of the hundreds around the various mission stations who are standing somewhere between the two kingdoms, convinced, though not converted, we cannot help coming to the conclusion that among the many agencies leading on to India's social and spiritual regeneration, these evangelistic efforts of missionaries form no unimportant part.

CHAPTER XII.

HAVE MISSIONS BEEN A FAILURE?

Success Twofold: (1) Individual Conversions: Converts, Their Steady Numerical Increase—Numerous Secret Disciples—Quality of the Converts. (2) Social Reformation: Loosening of the Bonds of Caste—Female Education—Widow Remarriage—Decay of Faith in Hinduism—Growth of Religious Fraternities—Christianity Has No Rival to Fear—Outlook for the Future.

WHAT success have Christian missions met with in South India? What is the present condition of society among the various classes of Hindus? What are the influences that reign amongst them? How far has contact with Christianity and Western civilization modified their social economy? Has caste lost any of its power? Have its degrading distinctions and observances fallen into decay? Do the superstitions of the ignorant still ride roughshod over the convictions of the enlightened? What is the evidence that the gospel is really leavening the mass of heathendom? Questions such as these suggest themselves to everyone interested in the well-being of the teeming millions of India. It is not our intention to answer these questions fully, but simply to point out some of the results of missionary effort, some of those social and religious changes which are more or less visible in Hindu society, and which indicate satisfactory and encouraging progress.

Missionary successes may be looked at from two standpoints: (1) Individual conversion; (2) social reformation.

1. When we look at the direct results of missions, we make bold to say that, so far from their having been a failure, success has largely attended them. The fallacy of Canon Taylor, in his recent article on the subject, consists in assuming that the ratio of progress is always the same, whereas the ratio of progress increases at a rapid rate. We are too apt to forget the power of the Spirit of God, the effect of pentecostal seasons of blessing, which are often the outcome of years of patient and earnest Christian toil. With regard to India, the Madras presidency has been, as yet, by far the most fruitful field of Protestant missions in that country. The following figures, taken from carefully-compiled statistics, will show the results which have been achieved between the years 1851 and 1881, when the last census was taken:—

	1851.	1881.
Native ordained agents	12	235
Native lay preachers	306	1,444
Native churches	161	2,758
Native Christians	74,176	299,742
Native communicants	10,334	70,607
Native contributions	rupees	82,902

The increase has been general over the whole field, but more markedly so in some parts than in others. The accessions have been most numerous among the lower classes and from the non-caste population, such as the Shanars, of Tinnevelly and Travancore, the Malas and Madigas of the Nellore and Cudappah districts, and the Pariahs of the Madura and North Arcot districts. In the villages the advance has been more rapid than in the towns. The higher castes and wealthy classes have resisted the truth stoutly; the actual converts from among these classes have been comparatively few, but as a rule they have been men of power, who have added strength and solidity to the Christian community.

There is no need to be ashamed of a gospel that has not laid hold of the upper and educated classes. The gospel thus spread at first. Intellectual revolutions begin at the top and filter down; religious revolutions begin at the bottom and rise, and it is always the "lower orders" that are laid hold of first. "Not many wise men after the flesh, not many mighty, not many noble, are called; but God hath chosen the foolish things of the world to confound the wise; and God hath chosen the weak things of the world to confound the things which are mighty." A devout and highly-educated native ministry is, however, one of the great and pressing needs of the country.

Then the results which appear are no measure of the results which have actually been attained.

There are large numbers of "secret disciples," men who, like Nicodemus, confess not Christ "for fear," who are kept back from public confession by fear of persecution and social ostracism. Who can estimate the numbers of these? We assert fearlessly that they are as many as, if not more than, the actual converts in South India at the present time. Till the acceptance of Christianity becomes more popular and general, the number of "secret disciples" will continue to be large. Elijah thought he was the one and only faithful man in the worst days of Ahab's reign, but, unknown to him, the Lord had rescued seven thousand men whose knees had not bent to Baal. Looking at the figures given above, and taking into account what cannot be given, who can deny that there has been real and marked success?

With regard to the quality of the converts, we believe that to an extent equal to that of the churches of our own country, they have honored that profession by a consistent walk and conversation. No doubt some have disgraced their confession. But was there nothing of that kind in the apostolic age? Did the apostle Paul never have to complain of those who had forsaken him, "having loved this present world?"

The native churches contain, it is true, men who are imperfect in knowledge, deficient in zeal, and scant in liberality, but, nevertheless, true men, who are struggling honestly and manfully against the vices and corruptions of the heathen society around them. In this respect they are not unlike the churches mentioned in the New Testament. Depreciators of mission work often look only at the weak side of converts, forgetting that many such converts were Christians in Ephesus, Corinth, and Colosse in the days of the apostles, and that the warnings and rebukes of the Epistles are exactly suited to the churches planted in the mission stations of South India in the present day.

Again, if Europeans see such miserable specimens of Christianity, the heathen on their part too often see such unhappy specimens of European Christians as to make them doubt the superiority of Christianity to their religions. It is a notorious fact that nowhere is there to be seen so low a type of Hindu Christianity as is to be found in those towns where it is brought most into contact with our own people. It is from seeing such as these that people speak contemptuously of native Christians, and imbibe a prejudice against missions. Strangely true, but most suggestive, is the fact that the most unsatisfactory native Christians are those engaged in employments which bring them much in contact with Europeans.

The best native Christians are those who live in small towns and villages remote from the large cities, and who have little or no intercourse with Europeans, except the missionary and his family. These exhibit a simple faith, a patience under suffering, a calm resignation to God's will, and a belief in the efficacy of prayer, not to be surpassed anywhere. These, and such as these, are "the joy and crown" of the missionary; they would be an honor to any Christian community, and are known to few Europeans.

Moreover, is it not true that in so-called Christian countries drunkenness and debauchery, violence and commercial dishonesty, attain large proportions, and that people apologize for this state of things by saying that good and evil, tares and wheat, will always be mingled in the world? May not the same be said with tenfold more force of native Christians, who have only recently emerged from the grossest ignorance and superstition? Anyhow, British or American Christians live in too large a glass house to make it advisable for them to throw stones at native Christians, and the latter will bear favorable comparison with the Christians of this or of any other country. Sir W. Muir, formerly lieutenant-governor of the Northwest Provinces, said, at the Reading Conference in 1883, "Thousands have been brought over, and in an ever-increasing ratio converts are being brought over, and they are not shams or paper converts, but good and honest Christians, and many of a high standard."

2. Looking now at the second standpoint from which missions may be viewed, namely, social reformation, one cannot fail to be struck with the mag-

nitude of the changes that have taken place. It is impossible to speak of native society without taking into account that withering institution, caste, which is unquestionably the most potent obstacle to the gospel, and the most resolute opponent to social progress and general enlightenment. It is the ax which has been laid at the root of all community of feeling, action, and aspiration. To keep his caste inviolate, to observe certain ceremonies, to propitiate the gods with offerings, is the whole duty of the Hindu. Obviously, the only way to perpetuate the distinctions of caste was to ignore, and as far as possible to obliterate, the moral sense, and to restrain all independent thought and action. This Hinduism has succeeded in doing for long ages, and its power would not even now have been impaired but for the entrance of a light which is fast dispelling the darkness of ignorance. Christianity, Western science and literature, and growing commercial interests, are the forces now arrayed against it; and the humiliations it has suffered within recent years may safely be regarded as indicating the final issue of the contest. Caste is only a part of the larger system of Hindu idolatry; and it would be strange if the truth which has in numerous instances broken the power of idolatry had not also loosened the hold of caste. A battery brought to bear on an enemy's stronghold may make a breach only on one spot; but the ceaseless cannonading may have had the effect of so shaking the walls of the fortifications as to render them useless for purposes of defense. In like manner, the damage which Christianity and education have done to the ramparts of Hinduism is greater in extent than the breaches that have been made. These forces have shaken the whole fabric—a fact which its defenders are the first to acknowledge. Superstition cannot flourish in the light of knowledge, and it can be easily understood how the enlightenment which is fast becoming general among the upper classes should have largely shaken their faith in the Vedas and Shastras. But while this revolution has been going on among the higher classes of the people, the other grades of society have had their faith in Hinduism greatly shaken by missionary education and preaching, and by the circulation of the Bible and other religious books. This is evident from the declining interest in the great annual festivals, and the complaints of the Brahmins that the gifts of the people and their reverence for the gods are not what they used to be, and also from the kind of reception now accorded to the messengers of the truth.

The movements in favor of female education and the widow remarriage question also illustrate the manner in which the moral influences abroad in the land are undermining the old constitution of native society. There is a comparatively strong party of educated and enlightened Hindus who are endeavoring to turn the tide of public opinion in favor of widow remarriage, and already a score or more of widows have been remarried. This party keeps up a ceaseless agitation on the subject, and by learned dissertations abounding in quotations from the Vedas and Shastras, by newspaper articles, by songs and dramas of varied merit, seeks to turn the tide of public sympathy in its favor. The agitation thus persistently kept up proves that they have not lost faith in their cause, or in the power of moral truth. It also illustrates the reality of the revolution that is overtaking Hindu society.

We have not yet had time to witness the results of this great department of missionary work, perhaps the most important department—the work of female education. In the female schools and in the mission to the zenanas lie the germs of a revolution such as India has not yet seen. There we go to the fountain-head, and when the home is pure, all will be pure. The battle of Christianity, we believe, will largely be fought out in the zenanas, in winning the women of India to Christ.

But not only are female education, widow remarriage, and the loosening of the bonds of caste among the beneficent influences now working in Hindu society, but the Hindu mind is in anxiety and concern about the moral and religious views, so opposed to its own way of thinking, which are shaking the foundations of native society. It is true that, while Hindus have been affected by the divine claims of Christianity, they do not generally accept it, yet it is also true that they have become very fearful on the subject of their own religion. Educated men in every town and city begin to perceive and acknowledge the untenableness of idolatry, and of the superstitions connected with it. They are impressed, also, with the low standard of morality fostered by their religion, and with the much higher standard enforced by Christianity.

The people are becoming ashamed of Hinduism. Stories of the vilest character which were formerly accepted as true are now explained away, and everything of a higher moral value is brought forth from the forgotten past to prop up a fast-failing cause. The thousands of copies of the New Testament and other Christian literature which have been circulated among the students of high schools and colleges have been moulding their minds and leavening their words, opinions, and thoughts, until at last there is growing up a school of men who let idolatry drop away from them, or with greater energy and principle fling it aside. A school of men have arisen who cannot sympathize any longer with the old institutions of their fathers, but who turn aside and feel a greater sympathy with Christian truth than with anything which has come down from their ancestors in the old time. But for the time being they are perplexed as to the right course to follow. It goes against the grain to abandon utterly the old faith and to embrace an alien creed. Christianity appears to them as an enemy to everything distinctively Hindu. They fail to see that it is universal, and not merely European. Hence many are endeavoring to carve out a new religion for themselves by adhering to certain primitive forms of Hindu belief, and expanding them so as to meet the necessities of modern Hindu thought. They are endeavoring to trace back the Hindu faiths to their purest sources, and to give the past a new fulfillment through the wider knowledge of the present. This is emphatically the attitude of the Hindu mind in South India at the present time.

Others, becoming eclectics, select prominent tenets from several creeds, especially from Christianity, gather up the whole into one, and so form a new religion, containing, as they suppose, the cream of all religions. Nevertheless, there is more honesty, more truth, more virtue, and more right religious feeling than there ever was. Not that the change in these respects is very distinctly manifest, for deceit and vice of many forms are still distressingly prevalent. But there is a wider, deeper sympathy with all that is pure and noble, holy and good, than ever existed before. Without doubt, India *is* responding to the potent touch of Christianity. We are not to consider the numerical insignificance of Christianity as compared with the population, but its vastness as compared with what the number of Christians was less than a hundred years ago. Far beyond the numerical strength of Christianity in South India, as indicated above, is the strength of the Christian position itself. Indeed, the comparatively small proportion of the Christian population to the whole makes it almost difficult to speak of it as one of the great religions of India, if it were not just for this fact, that it is evidently a living religion amidst the dead and the dying. The religious fraternities, which are springing up on all hands, are due to the elevating power of Christian principle. Just as the Gnostic heresies were among the factors of early Christianity, so we must reckon the Brahmas among the factors of modern Indian Christianity.

Though the educated Hindus do not readily embrace Christianity, yet their own religion is relaxing its hold upon them. Christian doctrine is almost universally assented to, but at present it is only in rare cases that the will is aroused to break away from the solid system of caste and custom which forms the social fabric. That this is a natural stage of transition from an ancient historic religion to Christianity, history abundantly testifies. The cultivated classes among the Greeks and Romans passed through such a period of skepticism, after the popular mythology had ceased to satisfy and before Christianity had secured its hold. The religious societies springing up in India are only fresh instances of a vague and unsatisfactory longing for something better than their old religion.

Looking, then, at the indirect results of missionary enterprise, such as the increased enlightenment of the people, the numerous reforms in their social condition as well as in their principles of action, the inquiries that are everywhere being made into the truths of the Christian religion, the universal acknowledgment of its superiority to their own religion in regard to the high morality which it inculcates, the laxity of large numbers, especially those educated in mission and government institutions, in the practice of idolatrous rites, the formation of religious fraternities like the Brahmo Somaj, etc., which are more or less patterned after Christianity, the prevalence of a desire to know and worship God as a Divine Father and Friend, no one can deny that the changes which Christianity and education have effected in the social and religious condition of the Hindus of South India are very great.

The old errors, delusions, and superstitions to which they have been wedded for long ages, are fast losing their hold on the sympathies of the educated classes, who on all sides are breaking away from the mental bondage in which they have for long years been enslaved. They are being more and more affected every year by English ways and manners, English civilization and life, and are conscious of the impartation of a new spirit and a new energy to their inner natures. The leaven is in the meal and the results are slowly and silently manifesting themselves.

The work of evangelization may seem to progress slowly to some eyes, but it is not really so, when we take into account the vastness of the population and the intense conservatism of the people. A handful of coloring matter thrown into a vessel of water colors it immediately, but to color a lake requires many a handful of coloring matter and much time. The apparent slowness of the progress of Christianity should, therefore, deceive no one. "The Lord is not slack concerning his promise, as some men count slackness." "One day is with the Lord as a thousand years, and a thousand years as one day."

The similarity between the condition of the country now and the state of the Roman world when the first ambassadors of the cross went forth to proclaim the gospel, has often been remarked. Widespread skepticism marked that period; intelligent and thoughtful men more than doubted the popular creed; the ancient moorings had parted; the ties of superstition had been loosened. Sects, such as the Gnostics and the Marcionites, sprang up, heathen in heart and origin, but acknowledging some of the truths of Christianity. Human thought began to center more and more around the person of Christ, till Christianity permeated the empire.

It is even so now to a large extent in South India. The first stage, when Christ and Christianity and everything connected with them were despised, hated, and, if possible, destroyed, has mostly passed away. A change has come over the thinking mind, which shows that the second stage has been entered upon. Hindus do not so much oppose Christianity as admit that some parts of it are worthy of being considered, and even embraced. They begin to acknowledge the truth and beauty of the moral teaching of the Bible. The idea of the one God that it presents is not distasteful. The one difficulty is Jesus Christ and his divinity. The storm is rapidly concentrating its strength and fury around his sacred person. The one question still to be settled is, "What think ye of Christ?" Christianity has no rival to fear. Mohammedanism cannot be called an aggressive religion, at least so far as South India is concerned. There are only two systems to our mind which seriously dispute the claims of Christianity to the allegiance of the people, viz., infidelity and Brahmoism.

Is it probable, then, that Hinduism will be supplanted by infidelity? We think we can answer decidedly in the negative. If the history of India teaches anything, it is that the Hindus are essentially a religious race. They banished Buddhism on account of its atheistic character, and they will never endure a negation of God and faith. Will, then, the passing away of Hinduism, and the vacuum left thereby, be filled up by Brahmoism? Here, also, the answer, it seems to us, is not doubtful. The influence of Brahmoism on the intelligent portion of Hindu society is becoming less and less. Ardent young students may join the sect and boast of its excellence, but the heads of families, the leaders of society, distrust it. Its shifting basis, its want of authority, and ignoring of those primeval traditions and yearnings which have characterized the Hindus throughout their whole history, doom it to failure. They have always felt the need of a divine revelation, a divine incarnation, and an atonement for sin; but Brahmoism offers them nothing but a total negation of these things.

Christianity, on the other hand, points them to the true revelation, the true incarnation, the true atonement for sin, and satisfies the deepest longings of their souls. No one can look at what has been already accomplished, and at what is now going on in South India, without acknowledging that Christianity is advancing in the land. If the present condition of the country had been predicted at the beginning of this century, it would have been pronounced an impossibility. The critic must be either ignorant of the facts or ignore them who does not see that the South India of to-day is no more the South India of seventy years ago than the Britain of to-day is the Britain of the last century.

There are, of course, some dark shades. There is the growth of intemperance. There is the spirit of indifference to all religions—the effect produced by the tone of much of our periodical literature, that all religions are equally good and equally bad, and that even Britain itself is becoming weary of its Christianity. There is the spread of infidel literature, the new birth of Hindu learning, and the wide dissemination of Hindu books through the printing-press. But we have no hesitation in saying that the time is coming when the whole of South India will be evangelized, and that neither Brahmoism nor Rationalism will be able to arrest its progress. It is not beyond the bounds of possibility that one effect of the new forces at work upon the religious conceptions of the country will be that a new religion will spring up. What form that new religion might take it is difficult to foresee. We do not think it is likely to be our modern Christianity, although Christian missions are at the present among the most powerful factors in determining what that new religion will be.

Sir William Hunter, in the *Nineteenth Century* for July, 1888, says: "I think it within reasonable probability that some native of India will spring up whose life and preaching may lead to an accession on a great scale to the Christian church. If such a man arises, he will set in motion a mighty movement whose consequence it is impossible to foresee."

This is always God's method of working. A long, slow, preparatory process, and then suddenly, when the fullness of time has come, a great harvest. We may expect to hear of whole tribes and communities abandoning their superstitions and embracing Christianity. There is no exaggeration in forming such anticipations. They rest on solid grounds. Great and efficient preparations have been made for securing them. Especially is there at the present time, not only in the city of Madras, but throughout nearly the whole of South India, an intense eagerness of thought on religious questions, reminding one of Milton's words, "A mighty and puissant nation arousing itself like a strong man after sleep." What is wanted is a pentecost—a fresh baptism of the Holy Spirit to touch the dry bones of heathenism.